Life in Genghis Khan's
Mongolia

Titles in The Way People Live series include:

Life in Genghis Khan's
Mongolia

by Robert Taylor

Lucent Books, CA 92198-9011

Library of Congress Cataloging-in-Publication Data

Taylor, Robert, 1948–
    Life in Genghis Khan's Mongolia / by Robert Taylor
        p. cm. — (The way people live)
    Includes bibliographical references and index.
    ISBN 1-56006-348-3 (lib. bdg. : alk. paper)
    1. Mongols—Juvenile literature. 2. Genghis Khan, 1162–1227—Juvenile litera-
ture. [1. Mongols. 2. Genghis Khan, 1162-1227.] I. Title. II. Series
    DS19 .T42 2001
    9.51'702—dc21

                                                        00-009685

Printed in the U.S.A.

Contents

Discovering the Humanity in Us All

Books in The Way People Live series focus on groups of people in a wide variety of circumstances, settings, and time periods. Some books focus on different cultural groups, others, on people in a particular historical time period, while others cover people involved in a specific event. Each book emphasizes the daily routines, personal and historical struggles, and achievements of people from all walks of life.

To really understand any culture, it is necessary to strip the mind of the common notions we hold about groups of people. These stereotypes are the archenemies of learning. It does not even matter whether the stereotypes are positive or negative; they are confining and tight. Removing them is a challenge that's not easily met, as anyone who has ever tried it will admit. Ideas that do not fit into the templates we create are unwelcome visitors—ones we would prefer remain quietly in a corner or forgotten room.

The cowboy of the Old West is a good example of such confining roles. The cowboy was courageous, yet soft-spoken. His time (it is always a he, in our template) was spent alternatively saving a rancher's daughter from certain death on a runaway stagecoach, or shooting it out with rustlers. At times, of course, he was likely to get a little crazy in town after a trail drive, but for the most part, he was the epitome of inner strength. It is disconcerting to find out that the cowboy is human, even a bit childish. Can it really be true that cowboys would line up to help the

cook on the trail drive grind coffee, just hoping he would give them a little stick of peppermint candy that came with the coffee shipment? The idea of tough cowboys vying with one another to help "Coosie" (as they called their cooks) for a bit of candy seems silly and out of place.

So is the vision of Eskimos playing video games and watching MTV, living in prefab housing in the Arctic. It just does not fit with what "Eskimo" means. We are far more comfortable with snow igloos and whale blubber, harpoons and kayaks.

Although the cultures dealt with in Lucent's The Way People Live series are often historically and socially well known, the emphasis is on the personal aspects of life. Groups of people, while unquestionably affected by their politics and their governmental structures, are more than those institutions. How do people in a particular time and place educate their children? What do they eat? And how do they build their houses? What kinds of work do they do? What kinds of games do they enjoy? The answers to these questions bring these cultures to life. People's lives are revealed in the particulars and only by knowing the particulars can we understand these cultures' will to survive and their moments of weakness and greatness.

This is not to say that understanding politics does not help to understand a culture. There is no question that the Warsaw ghetto, for example, was a culture that was brought about by the politics and social ideas of Adolf

Hitler and the Third Reich. But the Jews who were crowded together in the ghetto cannot be understood by the Reich's politics. Their life was a day-to-day battle for existence, and the creativity and methods they used to prolong their lives is a vital story of human perseverance that would be denied by focusing only on the institutions of Hitler's Germany. Knowing that children as young as five or six outwitted Nazi guards on a daily basis, that Jewish policemen helped the Germans control the ghetto, that children attended secret schools in the ghetto and even earned diplomas—these are the things that reveal the fabric of life, that can inspire, intrigue, and amaze.

Books in The Way People Live series allow both the casual reader and the student to see humans as victims, heroes, and onlookers. And although humans act in ways that can fill us with feelings of sorrow and revulsion, it is important to remember that "hero," "predator," and "victim" are dangerous terms. Heaping undue pity or praise on people reduces them to objects, and strips them of their humanity.

Seeing the Jews of Warsaw only as victims is to deny their humanity. Seeing them only as they appear in surviving photos, staring at the camera with infinite sadness, is limiting, both to them and to those who want to understand them. To an object of pity, the only appropriate response becomes "Those poor creatures!" and that reduces both the quality of their struggle and the depth of their despair. No one is served by such two-dimensional views of people and their cultures.

With this in mind, The Way People Live series strives to flesh out the traditional, two-dimensional views of people in various cultures and historical circumstances. Using a wide variety of primary quotations—the words not only of the politicians and government leaders, but of the real people whose lives are being examined—each book in the series attempts to show an honest and complete picture of a culture removed from our own by time or space.

By examining cultures in this way, the reader will notice not only the glaring differences from his or her own culture, but also will be struck by the similarities. For indeed, people share common needs—warmth, good company, stability, and affirmation from others. Ultimately, seeing how people really live, or have lived, can only enrich our understanding of ourselves.

Children of the Steppe

The continents of Europe and Asia share the largest plain in the world, a vast steppe, or grassland, that stretches five thousand miles from Hungary in the west to Manchuria in the east. From at least 4000 B.C., tribes of nomadic herders have struggled to wrest a living from this dry, flat wilderness. Relations between the tribes were volatile. At times, they formed alliances and lived together in harmony. Far more often, though, they were at war with each other, battling bitterly for control of grazing land to feed their animals.

The people who came to be known as the Mongols migrated into this cauldron of tribal strife during the eighth century. By the time Genghis Khan was born in the middle years of the twelfth century, conflict had become so intense and so frequent that the tribes were threatening to destroy each other.

Through military genius and political cunning, Genghis brought peace to the steppe by forging the combatants into a confederation with the Mongols in a position of unchallenged supremacy. From there, he led

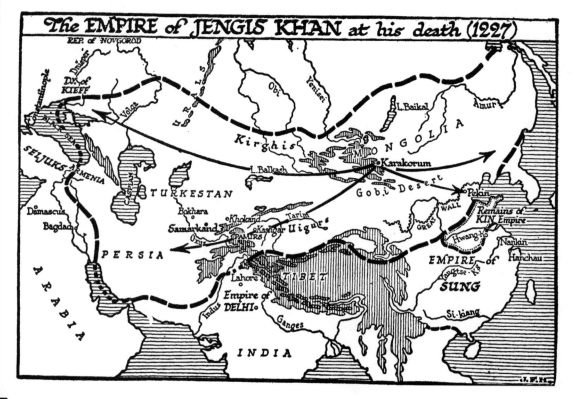

The EMPIRE of JENGIS KHAN at his death (1227)

his armies on campaigns of conquest that created the Mongol Empire, the largest dominion the world was to see until the British Empire circled the globe in the nineteenth century.

The Mongols' domain stretched from China to the borders of Russia and from the Persian Gulf to the Arctic Ocean and from it they accumulated a treasure-trove of plundered gold and jewels, but they remained children of the steppe. They possessed a warlike ferocity that baffled and horrified the civilizations they conquered. They prized loyalty, superstitiously worshiped nature spirits, and felt most fulfilled—most Mongol—when they were in battle. Their culture, social customs, and religious beliefs were shaped by the harsh geographic conditions of their homeland and the brutal economic realities of their pastoral-nomadic way of life. That way of life made the Mongols uncompromising and cruel, but it also made them durable, wise, and fascinatingly complex.

Nomads of the Steppe

No one knows the exact date of Genghis Khan's birth—the Mongols didn't keep records of such things because they didn't have a written language at the time—but most historians agree it was probably close to the year 1167. We know the details of his early life only because his son, Ogodei, later ordered a literate captive to write a biography, called *The Secret History of the Mongols*, to keep Genghis's memory alive for future generations.

Genghis's father, Yesugei, was the chief of a small and struggling clan of nomadic herders. He called his firstborn son Temujin, the name of a respected foe he had recently defeated in battle. Temujin's mother, Hoelun, was a member of the Tatar tribe, hereditary enemies of the Mongols. Following an age-old custom of the steppe, she became Yesugei's obedient wife after he abducted her from the Tatar man to whom she was betrothed.

Temujin enjoyed an uneventful childhood, described by the historian Paul Ratchnevsky: "Like all Mongol children, he learned to ride at an early age and practiced archery by shooting at birds. In winter he played on the ice of the Onon [River] with his brothers and other youngsters."[1]

When he was nine years old, the age at which marriages were arranged for Mongol children, his father determined he should become engaged to Borte, the ten-year-old daughter of an ally, and took him to meet his future in-laws. Leaving Temujin behind to get acquainted, Yesugei set out on the journey home. On the way, he encountered a band of Tatars who poisoned him to avenge the abduction of Hoelun. At the age of nine, Temujin inherited his father's title as clan chief.

Genghis's Rise to Power

Temujin's introduction to steppe politics was harsh, but it helped to mold him into the uncompromising leader he was to become. His clan refused to accept a chief so young and banished him and his mother, three brothers, and sister. Hoelun put up a spirited defense of her family, but her pleas fell on deaf ears and she was forced to feed them by grubbing for roots and snagging fish from the Onon River.

Despite the hardships, Temujin thrived during his years as an outcast and became a young warlord. Though he was just a teenager, he attracted a following of men who were convinced that under his charismatic leadership they would be able to enrich themselves by plundering their neighbors. He also claimed Borte as his bride, formed an alliance with another young warlord named Jamuka, and put himself and his band of raiders under the protection of Togril, a powerful steppe chief.

His wealth, measured in the size of his herd of horses, grew and so did his ambition. He won power struggles with both Jamuka and Togril and emerged as a force to be reckoned with among the warring clans and tribes of the steppe. Success came with a price, however. Borte was captured and raped by a group of marauding Tatars. Temujin eventually freed her and accepted as his own the son she bore nine months later. To the end of his life, he steadfastly defended the honor of his wife when others questioned the paternity of the child.

Soon, Temujin was the most powerful chief on the steppe. He incorporated conquered tribes into his army and by the year 1206 he had no equal. He summoned a grand council, called a quiriltai, and declared himself to be Genghis Khan—the Great Khan—with a divine mandate to rule the world. At that moment, the Mongol Empire was born.

The Cruel Steppe

The drama of Genghis Khan's rise to power was played out against the backdrop of one of the most inhospitable environments in the world. The Mongols lived on the eastern half of the Central Asian steppe, bounded to the north by the Siberian tundra and to the south by the Gobi Desert. It shares the extreme climate of both these regions, enduring arctic cold during nine-month winters, with temperatures plunging as low as –40 degrees Fahrenheit, and searing 100-plus degree heat in summer.

Most importantly, it is dry, far too dry to sustain an agricultural economy. This cold, arid, unfriendly land steeled the Mongol character and shaped the history of this hardy people. From the Stone Age until the present, steppe dwellers have been denied the luxury and security that farming provided for the civilizations that prospered on their borders. They were forced to turn first to hunting and then to herding to eke out a living. Ani-

mals rather than plants became their food supply, converting the sparse vegetation of the steppe, too coarse for human stomachs to digest, into edible protein.

The Mongols' economic existence was precarious, but it prepared them to become a peerless military power under Genghis's ruthless guidance. The unpredictable weather of the steppe caused frequent droughts. Acceptable pasture land was always a prize to be fought for and, once won, protected at the cost of life itself. Battle thus went hand in hand with herding and the Mongols came to regard it as a normal state of affairs.

The steppe is wide and for the most part flat, affording the Mongols and the other tribes who lived there ample opportunity to roam in search of good pasture. As historian

In 1206, Genghis Khan declared himself the ruler of the Mongol Empire.

David Christian says: "For communities of hunters or pastoralists, the steppe allowed great freedom of movement, almost as much as the sea did to seagoing societies."[2] This constant movement became an inescapable part of life. They were an entire society in perpetual motion, and Genghis used this mobility to great advantage in his wars of conquest.

Neighborhood Attractions

In their travels, the Mongols butted against the agricultural civilizations that surrounded them. They had the opportunity to observe and envy the better standard of living these peoples enjoyed and came to covet their material wealth and cultural accomplishments. They traded livestock and hides for grain, textiles, metals, and pottery, but they also realized their superior mobility and battle skills opened another door—that of plunder—and this too became part of the fabric of their lives.

They took what they wanted and retreated to the steppe, expressing little interest in the settled ways of their neighbors until the time of Genghis Khan's grandchildren. Raiding parties returned home with a wealth of plunder and stories about the wonders they had seen, but the Mongols didn't take their description further and learn the arts of agriculture. Their nomadic roots ran too deep to evolve beyond the culture they had inherited from their roving ancestors. Even when they invaded these sedentary civilizations, their goal was limited to exploiting what they found there to enhance their way of life, not change it. For them, wealth was ultimately measured in livestock and the pasture land required to keep their herds healthy and increasing in numbers.

A Killer Climate

Friar Giovanni DiPlano Carpini had to traverse the entire Central Asian steppe when Pope Innocent IV sent him to gather intelligence at the court of Genghis Khan's grandson Guyuk at the Mongol capital, Karakorum, in 1245. His description of the weather he encountered, which appears in *The Story of the Mongols Whom We Call the Tartars*, hardly reads like a travel brochure:

The weather there is extremely variable. In fact, in the middle of summer, when other areas have the greatest heat, there is a good deal of thunder and lightning which kills many people, and a great deal of snow actually falls there then. There are great cold windstorms too, so that often men can ride horses only with difficulty. Therefore when we came to the horde [as their emperor's and princes' camps are called] we had to throw ourselves flat to the ground because of the force of the wind, and there was so much dust we could hardly see. In winter, it never rains there, while in summer it often does, but so little that it can hardly soak the dust and roots of the pastures. Hail, by contrast, falls abundantly. Once, at the time chosen for the emperor to be enthroned, we were at the court and so much hail fell that when it suddenly melted, we understand that more than 160 people in the camp were drowned and many huts were swept away too. And in the summer there may suddenly be extreme heat and then suddenly extreme cold. During the winter in one area a very great deal of snow falls, while in another very little.

Historian Rene Grousset describes the dilemma that confronted the Mongols. On the one hand, they had the military might to conquer all that lay before them. On the other, they had little idea what to do with the new territories that came under their control. "On the threshold of these forays, where the steppes ended and cultivation began, [the Mongol] glimpsed a way of life very different from his own, one which was bound to arouse his greed," Grousset writes:

Especially in winter, his eyes turned toward the temperate lands of the south. . . . Not that he had any taste for cultivated land as such; when he took possession of it, he instinctively allowed it to relapse into a fallow, unproductive state, and fields reverted to steppe, to yield grass for his sheep and horses. Such was the attitude of Genghis Khan in the thirteenth century. Having conquered the Peking region [in China] his genuine desire was to raise the millet fields of the fair plain of Hopei to the dignity of grazing land. Yet, although the man from the north understood nothing of husbandry . . . he appreciated urban civilizations for their manufactured goods and their many amenities as objects of sack and plunder.[3]

Cowboys of the Steppe

In response to the harsh geographical conditions of their homeland, the Mongols had no choice but to evolve as a nomadic people. Their life was measured by seasonal migrations from pastures on the open steppe in summer to more sheltered grazing areas in

The Mongols were a nomadic people who depended on open pastures to feed their vast herds of livestock.

protected valleys during the bitterly cold winters. But the Mongol nomads didn't wander aimlessly in a never-ending random search for favorable living conditions. Their migrations were as carefully planned as large-scale military operations and the skills they learned in moving their vast herds of livestock stood them in good stead when they embarked on their wars of conquest. David Christian comments: "Pastoralist lifeways instilled some of the skills of logistics and scheduling necessary for a large campaign, for all pastoralists had to be able to schedule their migrations with some precision."[4]

Each group of Mongol herders controlled specific areas where they pastured their animals in summer and winter. They also controlled the routes that joined these areas. So Mongol migration had to be a meticulously thought-out undertaking—distances were carefully calculated by the chiefs, duties delegated, supplies secured, discipline maintained. Scouts were sent out to survey the territory to be crossed and they reported back on the activity of rival groups who might be contemplating a bid to take over the intended pasture site. They took a careful census of the potential opposition, and on that basis drew up contingency plans should a battle become necessary. Because every man, woman, and child had a role to play in this complicated logistic operation, the distinction between the sexes and age groups was blurred to a far greater degree than it ever was in any of the agrarian societies the Mongols came in contact with.

The nomadic way of life promoted self-sufficiency and adaptability. Unlike agricultural societies, nomads accumulate no economic surpluses to see them through hard times. Their survival depends on their ability to respond decisively and effectively to sudden changes in climate. If a usual pasture was dev-astated by drought or flood, they quickly had to find—and fight for—a new one.

Grousset highlights the degree to which the Mongols were shaped by their environment and hardened by the discipline of economic scarcity:

Never were men more sons of the earth than these, more the natural product of their environment; but their motivations and patterns of behavior acquire clarity as we come to understand their way of life. These stunted, stocky bodies—invincible, since they could survive such rigorous conditions—were formed by the steppes. The bitter winds of the high plateaus, the intense cold and torrid heat, carved those

The Mongols' tough physical appearance resulted from their ability to endure the harsh environment of the steppe.

A Mongolian woman milks her goat on an open pasture.

faces with their wrinkled eyes, high cheekbones and sparse hair, and hardened those sinewy frames. The demands of a pastoral life, governed by the seasonal migrations in search of pasture, defined their specific nomadism, and the exigencies of their nomadic economy determined their relations with sedentary peoples: relations consisting by turns of timid borrowings and bloodthirsty raids.[5]

The Mongol Menagerie

Mongol herds consisted of horses, cattle, sheep, camels, and goats. Of these, the horse was by far the most important to their way of life. Early visitors to their camps on the steppe were dazzled by the number of horses they saw—so many, said Friar Giovanni DiPlano Carpini, who witnessed the vast herds first-hand on his diplomatic mission from Pope Innocent IV in the year 1245, "that we did not believe there were that many in all the world."[6]

The horse was a lifeline for the Mongols because it provided not only meat and milk but also transportation, without which the rest of their economic, social, political, and military life would not have been possible. More than that, however, the horse was the universal symbol of prestige. The more horses a Mongol had, the higher his standing in the community. Horse breeders were regarded as the aristocrats of the steppe, with a more lofty social position than cattle or sheep breeders, with whom they often fought over grazing land, much in the same way cattle ranchers squabbled with sheep herders on the American western frontier.

It's not unfair to say that the Mongol lived on his horse. Describing an earlier era of steppe life, but one that changed little over the centuries, the Roman historian Ammianus wrote: "They remain glued to their horses, hardy but ugly beasts, on which they sometimes sit . . . to perform their everyday business. Buying or selling, eating or drinking, are all done by day or night on horseback, and they even bow forward over their beasts' narrow necks to enjoy a deep and dreamy sleep."[7] This state of oneness between the Mongol and his horse was one of the key ingredients in his military superiority.

Sheep were next in order of importance, providing mutton, milk, and cheese, the staples of the Mongol diet, and wool from which the women made felt for clothes and coverings for the walls and floors of their gers, the felt tents in which the Mongols lived. From cattle, they obtained additional meat, and both oxen and camels were used as beasts of burden. The goat ranked lowest, so low that the phrase "goat's foot" was widely bandied about as an insult, translating roughly as "worthless." The Mongols abhorred waste; nowhere was that frugality more evident than in their use of the dung their livestock left on the steppe in copious amounts. They dried it and burned it to heat their gers and cook their food.

The Mongol menagerie was rounded out by falcons, which were used for hunting and sport, and dogs, which earned their keep by guarding the herds and cleaning up the campsites by scavenging the few scraps of uneaten food the thrifty Mongols cast aside. Although there are references to dogs as pets of children, the practice was apparently not widespread. Because they were trained to attack on sight when minding the herds, dogs were too dangerous for children to play with; *The Secret History of the Mongols* reports that even Genghis Khan himself was afraid of them when he was a toddler.

The Seasonal Migration

When the time came to move the herds, the Mongols had an opportunity to showcase their amazing organizational skills. A typical migration involved hundreds of people and tens of thousands of animals. Mongol families, if they were on good terms with each other, allowed their herds to mingle, using brands to distinguish ownership. If there were alternate routes to the destination, a desirable situation since there would be more for the animals to eat along the way, the clan chief ordered the herd to be divided and assigned the most capable men to lead each part. He designated rendezvous points and established a strict time frame for each segment of the herd to arrive at them.

At the chief's command, the gers were broken down and loaded onto heavy wooden carts along with the meager possessions of each family. Each cart, pulled by oxen, was driven by an able-bodied woman and also contained those too young or old to ride. Everyone else—men, women, and children— was on horseback, each with a specific role to play in the animal drive. Some were scouts, others herded, still others swept the surrounding area for strays. Everyone carried a bow, sometimes two, and a quiver of arrows to fight off any raiders the party might encounter.

Each rider also carried enough provisions for the journey. These rations included dried milk curd, kumiss (fermented mare's milk, of which the Mongols were perhaps too fond), millet, and dried meat, which they tenderized by putting it under the saddles of their horses while they rode. The dried milk curd was mixed with water in a leather flask to produce a type of thin yogurt. The millet was also mixed with water to make a weak gruel.

The Mongol Mobile Home

When the Mongols moved, their homes moved with them. These ingenious structures are called gers, although they are better known as yurts, the name given to them in Siberia and among other nomadic peoples of the Asian steppe. They are still in use today.

The ger is a rounded, six-sided tent, supported by a collapsible lightweight wooden frame. This frame is covered with layers of felt, a heavy, weather-resistant fabric made of matted wool, held in place by leather straps. Often, the felt is treated with animal grease to further weatherproof it and a heavy felt door flap provides additional protection from the elements. The floor consists of planking covered with felt, except for a hearth in the center where the family burned dried animal dung for warmth and cooking fuel. Smoke from the fire escaped through a hole, or skylight, in the middle of the roof.

In the time of Genghis Khan, gers varied in size depending on the wealth of the owner. Some chiefs had separate gers for cooking, sleeping, and even "guest gers" for wayfarers. A modest family might live in a ger with a sixteen-foot diameter, while the tent of the Khan himself was an enormous floating palace capable of holding more than one hundred people. Some gers were taken down and folded up for travel, others were hoisted onto heavy ox carts and moved intact. An obviously impressed William of Rubruck, like Carpini another medieval European cleric on a mission to investigate the Mongol threat, reported: "I have counted to one cart 22 oxen drawing one house, eleven in a row across the width of the cart, and the other 11 in front of them. The axle of the cart was as big as the mast of a ship, and a man stood at the door of the house on the cart, driving the oxen."

A Mongol dismantles his yurt for traveling.

Along the way, this mobile city, for that's what it was, often encountered other groups engaged in similar migrations or caravans carrying goods between the sedentary civilizations of China and the West. These meetings provided an opportunity for trading and raiding. The caravans frequently transported commodities that the Mongols could not produce themselves—rice and grain, tea, textiles, and metal to make weapons. In exchange for these goods, the Mongols would trade livestock, leather, pelts, and furs, but the balance of trade, so to speak, was clearly in favor of the merchants. The Mongols needed their

Genghis Khan sets out on his annual hunt for game, an exercise that was also considered excellent military training.

wares more than the merchants needed what the Mongols had to offer. If they couldn't strike a reasonable bargain, the Mongols were quick to use their mobility and military skills to simply take what they wanted.

The Annual Hunt

Hunting was the second pillar on which the Mongol economy was based. The annual hunt was an event second in importance only to the seasonal migrations. The steppe people were descended from the savages who populated the Siberian forests to the north, whose survival depended solely on their hunting skills, and they married this culturally inherited ability with the military precision they brought to herding. Reversals of fortune or losing herds to famine or raids often reduced segments of the population to the same way of life that their forest ancestors pursued. In fact, it happened to the young Genghis Khan and his family when they were ostracized by their clan after the death of his father and forced to scratch out a living by hunting and fishing. The experience instilled a love of hunting in the Great Khan that continued until the end of his life. "We Mongols go hunting while we are still children," he proclaimed from his imperial throne. "This is a habit which I cannot renounce."[8] Indeed, the most generally accepted account of his death reveals that it was as a consequence of injuries he sustained after falling from his horse during a hunting expedition.

Like the seasonal migrations, the great annual hunt, or battue, was carried out every autumn with all the planning and gravity of a military operation. In fact, the Mongols used the hunt to practice military tactics and discipline, but its primary purpose was to supplement supplies of meat for the coming winter. Thousands of hunters were involved and the operation often took up to three months to complete.

After scouts were dispatched to scour the countryside in search of prey, under the direction of the leader, frequently Genghis Khan himself, the hunters proceeded in an orderly encircling maneuver, patiently and silently tightening the noose until the animals had no means of escape. Hunters who broke ranks were punished later with severe beatings.

Then, at the command of the leader, a fierce cry echoed across the steppe, the mounted hunters unleashed a barrage of arrows, and the slaughter began. Thousands of deer, bears—even tigers—were slain methodically and ruthlessly. After the hunt, every carcass was carefully counted and the spoils were divided among the leaders and subdivided down to the last man so that all partook in the bounty.

The Persian historian Juvaini was struck by the enormous scale of the hunt and the importance that Genghis Khan placed on it as a way to practice military tactics. Juvaini commented shortly after Genghis's death that the Khan

paid great attention to the chase and used to say that the hunting of wild beasts was a proper occupation for the commanders of armies; and that instructions and training therein was incumbent on warriors and men-at-arms, who should learn how the horsemen come up with the quarry, how they hunt it, in what manner they array themselves and after what fashion they surround it according as the party is great or small. For when the Mongols wish to go ahunting, they first send out scouts to ascertain what kinds of game are available and whether it is scarce or abundant.[9]

"Ugly Little Horses"

Like its owner, the Mongol horse was bred for performance, not appearance. Foreign observers were apt to scoff at the shaggy, short-legged, bull-necked little mounts—until they saw them in action. The Roman chronicler Ammianus described them as "ugly little horses, as tireless and swift as lightening."

The Mongol horse is an ancient breed. First domesticated in southern Russian more than thirty-five hundred years ago, it became renowned for its speed and stamina. It had short, powerful legs, making it surefooted on all types of terrain, and a thick coat to withstand the brutal winters of the steppe. Just as their tough riders ate in the saddle, the horses grazed as they moved from encampment to encampment, often rooting beneath the snow for the scrubby grass that formed the bulk of their diet.

The Mongols preferred to ride mares so they could drink their milk during long treks and outfitted their mounts with sturdy wooden saddles and short stirrups to maintain a solid seat during high-speed chases and the abrupt turns required by hunting and warfare.

Constant Battle

The Mongols' economic life equipped them to be the fierce warriors Genghis needed to create his empire. Scarcity toughened them, nomadism made them mobile, herding honed their riding skills, and hunting perfected their renowned ability as mounted archers. Both the seasonal migrations and the annual hunt instilled the fundamentals of military tactics.

Constant battle, both with rival tribes on the steppe and with bordering farming communities, hardened them to the horrors of war and the sacrifices that soldiers have to make in battle. It also stunted their sense of the sanctity of life—existence on the steppe was brutal and often short.

The Mongol herders provided Genghis with the perfect raw material to mold into one of the greatest armies the world has ever seen.

CHAPTER 2

Families, Clans, and Tribes

The rigors of their economic existence had turned the Mongols from hardy herders into natural soldiers, but before Genghis Khan could weld them into a fighting force to carry out his imperial dreams he had to overcome one monumental obstacle: The warring tribes of the steppe were not a unified nation. The task of unification was enormous because the hatred between the tribes sometimes went back generations and avenging past wrongs was a matter of honor.

The society into which Genghis was born was hierarchical. At the bottom were individual families. These were joined together in clans, which in turn made up tribes. However, two aspects of Mongol life clouded this relatively simple picture. The first of these was exogamy; that is, a man was required to marry outside his own tribe. The second was polygamy; a man could have as many wives as he could support. Husband and wife, therefore, could belong to tribes who were at war with each other. Alternatively, a man's family could include wives whose tribal loyalties put them in opposition. Further complicating this social landscape, where relationships were based on kinship, were two important traditions that cut across tribal affiliations. The first was blood brotherhood, whose ties were even stronger than those of blood, and the second was voluntary vassalage, in which a man chose to put himself in servitude to the chief of a clan or tribe other than his own.

The combined stresses of this network of relationships had reduced Mongols and the other tribes of the steppe to a state of anarchy that was threatening their very survival. The Persian historian Juvaini presents a vivid description of the dismal circumstances that prevailed: "They had neither ruler nor leader. The tribes lived apart, singly or in twos; they were not united and were either at war or in a state of suspended enmity with each other . . . and lived in abject poverty; they wore the skins of dogs and mice, ate the flesh of these and of other dead animals."[10]

That roughly describes conditions as Genghis Khan found them when he began his program to unify the fragmented peoples of the steppe into a coherent whole.

The Over-Extended Family

The Mongol family was definitely not nuclear in design. Due to exogamy and polygamy the typical family was really several families in one; each wife had her own brood of children and each of these "subfamilies" had ties of culture and kinship to a tribe different from that of the husband. In addition, grandparents and even in-laws could swell the family ranks and require the maintenance of several gers. In fact, anthropologists have found the word "family" to be inadequate and David Christian has proposed replacing it with the term "parental group."[11]

The typical polygamous Mongol family consisted of several families, including the wives' grandparents and in-laws.

This potential powder keg was held in check by rules and social conventions that imposed a semblance of order and structure. The first wife took precedence over the others and her children over theirs when the question of succession and inheritance arose. But this custom was all too often ignored, according to historian David Morgan, who explains that when the head of a family died "his effective successor might well be that one of his family who had succeeded in wiping out all the other contenders."[12]

What harmony there was depended on the restraint of the wives who were expected to keep jealous rivalries in check even when their respective tribes were sworn enemies. Men acquired wives in one of two ways: Marriages were arranged between young children to forge or strengthen tribal alliances, as in the case of Genghis Khan and Borte, or men captured women in raids on tribes with which they were at war, as in the case of Genghis's father and mother.

This phenomenon of wife stealing was widespread and enabled powerful chiefs to accumulate sizable harems and, often, hundreds of children. The family ranks were also swelled by adoption. It was a rigorously observed custom that the children of allies who fell in battle should be well cared for, and Genghis himself acquired four such adopted sons during the course of his life. Although neither they, nor the children of any of his numerous wives other than Borte, figured in his succession, they were treated the same as his natural children in every other way.

Inheritance also clouded this already-confusing picture. When a Mongol man died, his herds and possessions were divided among his sons, with the oldest getting those animals and grazing lands farthest from the family's home base. Intermediate sons inherited land and herds progressively closer to the family's traditional heart land, but the youngest son wound up with the homestead—and all of his father's wives except his mother. Thus, it was a common occurrence for a man to be the husband of his stepmother and the adoptive father of his stepbrothers and -sisters.

Clans

The clan (oboq) was the next level of Mongol social organization, but the line dividing it from the family was not a clear one. Because they incorporated so many elements, families also had some clan characteristics. Nevertheless, the clan, which was made up of several parental groups each headed by related men, was the basic unit of Mongol society. Comprising hundreds of people, the clan was responsible for the fundamental aspects of economic, political, military, and social life. Each clan was divided into subgroups that often traveled together on seasonal migrations.

Each of these subgroups chose a leader (batur) from among the eligible men, based on administrative ability and prowess in battle rather than seniority or kinship. "There had to be an accepted arbitrator for the resolution of disputes; there was need of a war leader in whom the warriors had confidence," writes David Morgan. "So chiefs were made not simply born."[13]

Clan councils made decisions concerning migratory routes and raids on neighboring tribes to replenish the herds. The clan chief

Who Were the Mongols?

Answering the question "Who were the Mongols?" provides insight into the complexity of the world Genghis Khan and his contemporaries lived in.

The first record of the Mongols as a distinct people occurs in the Tang dynasty of China between the years 618–907, some two hundred to six hundred years before Genghis unified the tribes of the steppe. They were called Menku and they lived by hunting in northeast China. Reportedly, they had not yet learned how to cook their food, but they were respected for their keen eyesight and other hunting skills. In fact, the word *Mongol* originated in a Chinese dialect and means "brave fighter who knows no fear."

Historians have not been able to pinpoint their origin more precisely than that, stumbling over the obstacle that there were no fewer than nine separate tribes with that name vying for supremacy in the same area.

However, sometime during the eighth century, Genghis Khan's ancestors began to migrate to the west and learned the art of animal husbandry on their way to their new home on the Mongolian plateau of Central Asia, where they still live today.

By the twelfth century, they shared—uneasily—the territory with a number of other tribes, the most prominent of among which were the Tatars, the Merkits, and the Naiman. It's ironic to note that the term *Tartar*, by which all these peoples came to be known in Europe, is derived from the name of the Tatars, who were the sworn enemies of the Mongols proper.

It was Genghis Khan's achievement to unite these tribes into one powerful empire, numbering about 3 million people. Thus the Mongols, as they have come to be known, are really a confederation of tribes, held together for a time by the iron will of Genghis Khan.

enjoyed supreme authority in time of war, but in peacetime he was expected to stay out of the business of individual families unless they invited him to settle conflicts. Other decisions, including those concerning migratory routes and raids, were made collectively at clan council meetings.

The chief meted out punishment for serious offenses, including theft from a fellow clansman and adultery, which was defined as illicit sex within the clan—one clansman having sex with another clansman's wife, for example. (It was perfectly acceptable for a man to have sex, even rape, a woman who was not attached to one of his relatives since this was unlikely to lead to clan strife.) Both of these crimes were punishable by death if the chief so decided.

Often, larger groups of clans and subclans, including those belonging to friendly tribes, gathered during the winter in shared protected pastures. At these times clan members exchanged news, discussed long-range plans, arranged and consummated marriages, forged alliances, and settled disputes—if they were of the sort that could be settled peacefully. The composition of these larger groups changed from year to year as clan fortunes rose and fell due to war or drought and they tended to be unstable in character. Intertribal warfare muddied the waters of clan life. Whole families were often captured, separated from their kinfolk, and incorporated into the victorious tribe. They often even took the name of their new masters. Families also were divided when women and children were captured and enslaved. Sometimes whole subclans became vassal clans of another tribe and were forced into combat against their relatives. Others

During harsh winters, Mongolian tribes gathered together to conserve and pool resources.

voluntarily put themselves under the protection of a powerful rival to escape the wrath of an enemy

Tribes and Supertribes

Clans were linked in larger tribal groupings (ulus), theoretically based loosely on kinship, but more often ad hoc alliances of the clans, brought together by the need to defend themselves against enemies or undertake a large-scale military operation to replenish depleted herds. Often, these alliances crossed cultural barriers and brought together people who spoke different languages.

Despite these differences, members of a tribe were intensely loyal to each other and frequently hostile to outsiders. They regarded their shared interests as paramount and often invented mythological ancestors to provide a blood relationship where none in fact existed. Because tribes were alliances of clans, they sometimes lacked strong individual leadership and were governed instead by councils of clan chiefs. Their ability to act in a unified manner was diminished in these cases, contributing to the chaos that was rampant in the twelfth century.

The Tatars were the most powerful tribe on the steppe at the time of Genghis Khan's birth. However, says Morgan, "they did not dominate, much less rule, Mongolia. . . . Since there was nothing that even approximated to a 'central government,' and because the tribal structure was apparently in something of a fluid state, circumstances were propitious for a successful young nomad warrior to build up a following of his own."[14]

Genghis Khan was astute enough to realize that tribes would coalesce around a strong leader and he exploited this aspect of their history to unify them into the supertribe that became the Mongol Empire. "The tribe was a rather 'open' institution," Morgan notes, "its membership created more by shared political interests than by descent from a common ancestor. It is only in this way that Genghis Khan was able to organize the nomads of Central Asia, an extraordinarily disparate collection of groupings whether considered 'racially' or linguistically, into a unified and effective war machine."[15]

Class

Class, social stratification based on wealth, also played a role in Mongol life. The nomadic herders didn't use money; rather, they counted their riches in the size of their herds of animals, particularly horses. Those with the largest herds were considered superior to those with fewer animals. These inequalities were negligible during times of scarcity because drought and famine affected rich and poor alike. The more horses one had, the more one would lose without sufficient food to keep them alive.

Class distinctions tended to be sharper during times of war. Families with the largest herds could afford to field the largest raiding parties and hence garner more spoils. Because it was common practice to capture members of defeated tribes and turn them into serfs and slaves, the households of these powerful families grew faster than others and social inequalities increased more rapidly. Eventually, certain families came to dominate the tribes to which they belonged. "The tribes had their noble families," David Morgan writes. "Genghis Khan himself was a member of such a family, some of whom had been powerful khans in earlier years. This was enough to make him a possible candidate for chieftanship."[16]

Serfs and slaves were forced to perform the more grueling menial tasks of day-to-day life. Their masters put them to work tending the herds, mending the gers, and making arrows and other weapons. They also used them in battle, putting them in the front ranks to endure the worst of the enemy onslaught. They became, in effect, the Mongol equivalent of cannon fodder.

Serfs were bound to their masters, but could own personal property. Slaves owned nothing and the slave population contained a large number of women, who were forced to become the concubines of their owners. A sad fact of Mongol life is that it included many slave children. Most of these were captives, but many were sold by impoverished parents into slavery. One story survives of a poverty-stricken tribesman who sold his child to Genghis Khan for a haunch of venison. In the words of *The Secret History*, the unfortunate man said: "I am in a strait. Give unto me a [morsel] from the flesh of that wild beast. I shall give unto thee this my child."[17]

In addition to herd and household size, markings of rank included more ornate gers, captured gold and jewelry, and other trappings of prestige. "Inequalities were also apparent in clothing," says David Christian. "While greater lords dressed in furs . . . and undergarments of silk, the poor used outer garments of from the hides of dogs or goats."[18]

Vassals

Voluntary vassalage, another traditional aspect of steppe life, played a key role in reinforcing class differences in Mongol society during the turbulent years of Genghis Khan's youth. A young Mongol man could, and often did, detach himself from his clan and join that of another, more powerful leader. The motive was twofold. First, a more powerful clan would offer him, his family, and his herds greater protection from enemies. Second, being part of a stronger clan extended the promise of greater wealth through the opportunity to share in the larger troves of booty that would inevitably accrue to those with superior military might.

These men became vassals—the Mongol word was nokod—willingly relinquishing their rights as independent individuals to serve a master. For the duration of their vassalage, they were second-class members of Mongol society. They did their master's bidding without question. If they disobeyed, they were punished by banishment or, if their offense was deemed serious enough, death. In times of battle, they fought as ordinary cavalrymen. In times of peace, they did menial tasks, much like slaves. However, unlike slaves, they could own property and they shared in the spoils of war. Most im-

Mongol Customs

Despite their well-deserved reputation as rapacious marauders, Mongol customs and morality were based on sharing, a discipline forced upon them by the economic scarcity that was an ongoing feature of their lives and a constant fear even when times were good. Generosity was prized as a virtue, as was loyalty and truth telling. Treachery and lying about important matters were both punishable by death and Genghis Khan did not hesitate to administer stern justice in these matters, often executing enemy soldiers who betrayed their leaders even though he used the information they provided to his advantage.

To seal their relationship, blood brothers often exchanged valuable items such as horses.

portantly, they could quit their servitude at any time.

"The nokod were freemen; they entered the service of a leader voluntarily and could leave him and attached themselves to another," Ratchnevsky writes. "They lived in their leaders household and were maintained by him. The nokod were constantly with their leader; in war they protected him from the enemy and guarded him while he slept; in peace they undertook household tasks."[19]

When he was a young and rising warlord, Genghis himself became a vassal when he offered his services to Togril and subordinated himself and his followers to the older potentate. There was, of course, an element of risk in this. If Togril's fortunes had ebbed before Genghis was strong enough to stand on his own, he would have been swallowed up by the ranks of a victorious tribe and would never have had the opportunity to extend his own influence. Before that could happen, however, his power grew to exceed that of his steppe lord and the positions were reversed, with Togril becoming his grateful vassal.

Brothers in Blood

Both Genghis Khan's life in particular and Mongol life in general were influenced by an institution that took precedence over all other social ties—blood brotherhood. In the Mongol language, the term for blood brother is *anda* and its importance cannot be overemphasized. Blood brotherhood sealed lifelong alliances and often dictated the relationships between entire tribes. Mongol society and history cannot be understood unless blood brotherhood is put in proper perspective.

The best way to do this is to take a page out of Genghis Khan's own life story. When, as a boy, he befriended Jamuka, they became andas. To seal their pact, they exchanged items that were of value to Mongol children. In his biography of Genghis, Ratchnevsky recounts:

These two boys were linked by a close friendship. . . . They made a compact of blood-brothership by exchanging knuckle bones, and, then, in spring, Jamuka gave Temujin a whistling arrow which he had made and received an arrow whose head Temujin had carved from juniper wood. The oath, to maintain eternal friendship, was strengthened by drinking from a beaker in which a few drops of blood of the new brothers had been mixed.[20]

When they were older, Temujin and Jamuka renewed their oath by giving each other horses and booty they had captured in their raids and forged an alliance that was to change the history of the steppe. They joined forces and began a series of campaigns against other nomadic tribes, eventually cementing the foundation of what would become the Mongol Empire. However, as their power increased they came to regard each other as rivals and when they had a serious falling-out it was one of the most traumatic experiences of Temujin's early life. It was only with the greatest difficulty, and after many delays and much soul-searching, that he made the fateful decision to have Jamuka executed for failing to provide promised support during a raid and leaving Temujin and his troops in a vulnerable position that could have cost them their lives.

It is eloquent testimony to the strength of the bond that existed between andas that even when Jamuka realized that Temujin was about to have him killed for his treachery, he

Rather than expand the Mongol territory collectively, many tribes repeatedly fought one another for the same territory.

pledged to support his blood brother from beyond the grave. In the words of *The Secret History*, we read this speech from Jamuka, as he waited for Temujin to pass the death sentence on him: "If thou, mine anda, favor me, if thou make me to pass away swiftly, anda, thou wilt be at peace as to thy heart. . . . When I shall die and shall lie in my grave . . . for ever and ever I shall offer protection unto the seed of thy seed—I shall become a prayer."[21] Though Temujin was furious with Jamuka, he honored his anda's last request and, according to the Mongol custom acknowledging a valiant adversary, had him executed quickly without spilling his blood on the ground and allowed his body to be buried on a hill, a place of honor for the revered dead.

A Dream of Union

Genghis Khan was deeply affected by the disorganization of the society in which he lived. He despaired over the senseless slaughter caused by intertribal warfare, not because he was offended by war itself, but because it all seemed to lead nowhere. Rather than improving the lot of all the Mongols, the tribes were destroying themselves and each other, taking and retaking the same territory over and over again as their fortunes rose and fell.

It was one of his greatest insights to realize that they were fighting over crumbs while ignoring a much greater prize. He came to believe that what the Mongols needed to do to survive and prosper was to stop fighting among themselves and turn their attention to the wealth that existed in the rich agriculture-based countries that bordered the steppe.

He began to dream of a vast army of Mongol warriors—with himself at its head, of course—that would sweep through these countries, plunder their wealth, and turn their lands into endless pasture for herds that would grow forever. By the start of the thirteenth century, he was well on his way to achieving that goal.

CHAPTER 3
Genghis's Reforms

Genghis Khan was an astute politician. He realized that the strength of the Mongol people lay in their nomadic way of life. It made them tough and mobile, providing them with the prerequisites for success on the battlefield. Though he dreamed of conquest, he never conceived that they would ever leave the steppe. He coveted the luxuries of the civilizations he hoped to conquer, but not their soft and settled way of life.

He also knew that however fractious and chaotic tribal life had become, he would never replace it with any other form of social organization. He was proud of his own tribal heritage and realized how ties of kinship increased the Mongols' sense of security and identity. But he was aware that without strong central leadership, the Mongols would be condemned to squander their resources on internal conflict.

Genghis felt that he was destined to be the leader who would save the Mongols from self-destruction. To achieve that goal, he wanted to preserve what was best about them—the nomadic economy and tribal social structure—but create a framework in which these institutions would work harmoniously. To that end, he instituted a series of reforms he hoped would hold tribal animosities in check and enable him to harness the military potential he saw all around him and turn it outward against the non-Mongol world.

The Yasa

After the tribes accepted him as their universal leader in the year 1206, Genghis's first order of business was to pass a series of laws. He hit on an ingenious idea: The Mongols were accomplished in the arts of war, so why not attempt to impose military discipline on the society at large?

The laws that Genghis promulgated to achieve this end were recorded by scribes in a large blue book called the Great Yasa. No copy of this book has ever been found. David Christian believes Genghis got the idea for the Yasa from a member of the conquered Naiman tribe, who, unlike the Mongols, had already adopted the Uighur written language. "Amongst those captured after the defeat of the Naiman in 1204, there was a literate official, Tata-tonga, who kept the official seals of the Naiman khan," Christian explains:

> The Naiman already had a script. It was probably Tata-tonga who persuaded Genghis Khan to introduce the same script for the writing of Mongolian. He also convinced Genghis Khan of the need for a more formal promulgation of laws, and the importance of written laws and seals. In 1206, Genghis Khan made his adopted son Shigi-khutugu, a sort of keeper of the laws.[22]

The essence of the Yasa was to take customary tribal practice and extend it to embrace all the tribes that made up the empire that Genghis was trying to build. For example, it was a revered social practice to extend hospitality to a member of one's own tribe. Under the Yasa, this became an obligation that each Mongol must extend to all others, regardless of tribe affiliation. As noted, adultery was forbidden among people who were bound to each other by ties of kinship. In Genghis's new legal framework, this prohibition applied across the society as a whole. The Yasa functioned both to regulate relations between individual Mongols and as a blue print for running the army and governing the empire.

The laws were harsh. Says historian Rene Grousset:

> The code was severe indeed: it demanded the death penalty for murder, major theft, concerted falsehood, adultery, sodomy, malicious witchcraft, receiving of stolen goods. . . . Disobedience, whether civil or military, was equated with crimes under common law, the yasa being at once a civil and administrative code: a discipline valid for the government of the world.[23]

From Tribe to Empire

As he was promulgating his laws, Genghis Khan also began to modify the concept of the tribe to suit his imperial ambitions. The system he hit on was based on the number ten. In this new scheme, ten families were organized into a group called an arban. Ten arbans consitituted a group of one hundred families called a jaghun. Ten jaghuns composed a one-thousand-family assemblage called a minghan, which effectively became a new type of tribe.

In many cases, a minghan was made up largely of families who already had traditional tribal ties. This was particularly true when Genghis was sure of their loyalty to his leadership. In other cases, though, the minghans were made up of families from many different clans and tribes. Genghis took this option when the original tribes had been his enemies and were incorporated into the empire only because his army had conquered them. In this way, he diminished the power of antagonistic clan-tribal chiefs and lessened the potential for revolt.

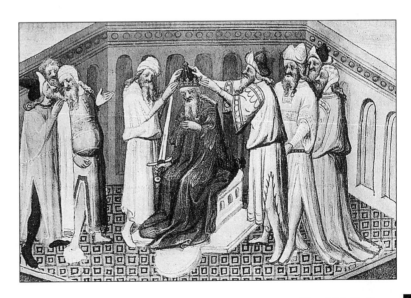

Soon after his rise to power, Genghis Khan created the Yasa, a group of laws designed to ensure tribal loyalty to him.

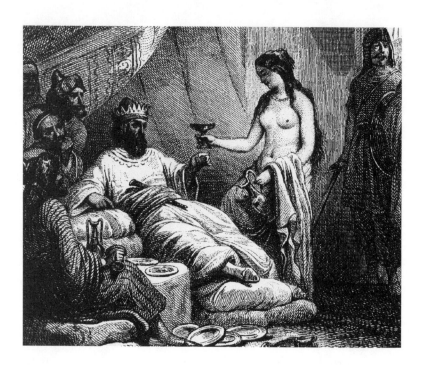

A new wife was added to Khan's family after each successful military campaign.

The leaders of these new groupings were recruited from among Genghis's faithful nokod. Since each of the groups provided fighting men for the imperial army, these nokod played a triple role: They were simultaneously tribal chiefs, military commanders, and imperial officials. Genghis thus organized all of Mongol society on military lines and, in so doing, created an army and an imperial bureaucracy of unprecedented power and discipline.

Charles J. Halperin, in a study of the success of the Mongol Empire's subjugation of Russia in the years immediately following Genghis's death, pays tribute to the masterful way in which the Great Khan integrated

> clan-tribal . . . and imperial social structures and political institutions. A single Mongol might be simultaneously a feudal vassal, a clan aristocrat and a bureaucratic official. The clan-tribal nomadic base was perpetuated even as the aristocratic elite

assumed new military, political and bureaucratic responsibilities. The fusing of identities and meshing of systems and forms gave cohesion to the empire, and the passage of time proved its viability.[24]

From Warlord to Emperor

Genghis Khan boasted of his fondness for the plain, unadorned life of the steppe, proudly declaring that he dressed in the same rough style and ate the same meager meals as everyone else. He was quick to disparage the luxury and self-indulgence he saw in the civilizations on the Mongols' borders and made lengthy speeches about the decay that would infect his people if they ever forgot their nomadic roots. However, Genghis was caught up by the forces he unleashed when he set out to transform the warring tribes into an empire under his command.

As his power grew, so did the complexity of his life, and an imperial court sprung up around him. It all started out simply enough. The young warlord first acquired an entourage comprising his wife Borte, their children, and a few nokod who had attached themselves to his rising star in the hope that his military prowess would bring them riches in the form of booty and stolen herds. But with each successful battle, the population grew.

New serfs and slaves were added. He brought back a new wife from each campaign and so the number of children also began to burgeon. The gers began to multiply. The herds increased. Success bred success and new nokod came to join his increasingly powerful band of marauders. Shamans, some less scrupulous than others, flocked to offer advice and blessings in exchange for a share in the loot.

Genghis's aspirations turned from plunder to politics and he began to dream of conquering entire nations. As his appetite for conquest grew, so did his needs. Despite his nostalgia for the simple life, he had set himself on a path that was to consign those days to memory. The steppe chief became an emperor and his ragtag entourage a full-fledged imperial bureaucracy.

The Floating City

By the time Genghis consolidated his power, his court had reached monumental proportions. He was well on his way to accumulating his final total of five hundred wives. His personal bodyguard consisted of ten thousand men, many with their own families in tow. The demands of ruling an empire that would grow to four times the size of Alexander the Great's required a bureaucracy of scribes, tax collectors, ambassadors, and administrators.

All of these people were obligated, according to the customs of the steppe, to support themselves with herds of horses and cattle and flocks of sheep and goats. All of them lived in gers and those who had multiple wives needed multiple gers. Genghis's band had grown into a small city.

But one thing hadn't changed—and wouldn't as long as Genghis was alive. The Mongols were nomads and that meant they moved constantly. The imperial court, despite the ponderous size to which it had grown, remained a nomadic household, always on the march. Wherever the Khan's lust for conquest took him, this entire mobile tent city followed.

Thousands of gers had to be broken down and loaded onto carts; hundreds of thousands

Women and Politics

Genghis Khan acknowledged the right of women to influence the Mongol political arena. While he was alive, the strength of his personality and his uncanny ability to judge character—and the terror he inspired—kept palace intrigue to a minimum, but after he died the politically ambitious had a field day. Oghul Qaimish, the widow of his grandson Guyuk, assumed the throne as regent following her husband's death and began to machinate for her son, Qucha. In this, she was opposed by another formidable Mongol woman, Soyurghaqtani, the widow of Genghis's youngest son, Tolui. A bitter power struggle ensued and Oghul Qaimish proved no match for her rival. She paid a heavy price for her foray into the cutthroat world of Mongol court infighting—she was publicly stripped naked, stitched into a carpet and trampled to death by horses.

of animals had to be herded along the proposed route; infants and the elderly had to be transported; booty, food supplies, and court records had to be packed up. Amid this swarming hive of activity sat the austere Khan, mounted on his horse, surveying the proceedings. At his command, hundreds of couriers scurried with instructions to herders overseeing the livestock, squads of armed scouts rode ahead to secure the way, military officers organized their cavalry troops into orderly ranks. Then, with a nod, he set this metropolis in motion, every part meshing like gears in a vast machine.

Down to Business

In certain respects, the Mongol Empire was Genghis Khan's family business, and that business was war and plunder. Much of court life was devoted to plotting and planning military campaigns and devising ever more ingenious ways to extract taxes and tribute from conquered peoples. With the Great Khan himself as chief executive officer and chief operating officer, proponents of competing strategies argued for their points of view. A conservative faction, adhering to the traditions of the steppe, tried to persuade the Khan to adopt a slash-and-burn policy with respect to foreign territories: Steal the livestock, plunder the material wealth, kill the populace and turn the land into pasture for the growing herds. A more progressive group, influenced by the foreign cultures they had observed, countered with the point of view that conquered people should, of course, be plundered and subjugated, but be left just enough material resources to pay taxes and tribute on a continuing basis.

There is no doubt about where Genghis's heart lay. He was fond of issuing pronouncements from his throne on the issues brought before him. Called biliks, these declarations were faithfully recorded by his scribes. One day, as the debate droned on, he rose from his seat and silenced the assembled advisers by stating his personal definition of what it was to be a Mongol: "to cut my enemies to pieces, drive them before me, seize their possessions, witness the tears of those dear to them, and

Despite its size, the Mongol empire remained a mobile community.

The Mongols had nothing approaching a city during Genghis Khan's lifetime; his devotion to the nomadic life of the steppe refused to allow it. However, he did have a winter camp near the Orkhon River, about 150 miles from the present-day Mongolian capital of Ulan-Bator. On that site, his son, Ogodei, established Karakorum in the 1230s and tried to set up his court there on a more or less permanent basis. It never really caught on—the nomadic roots ran too deep—and by the time William of Rubruck visited in the 1250s, it was little more than a trading center. Yet, he described a fairly cosmopolitan town, with an active marketplace and an area where foreign craftsmen plied their various trades. It had two mosques and one Christian church as well as twelve temples devoted to the worship of native dieties. It was enclosed by a mud wall with four gates at which various merchants peddled grain and livestock. Most significantly, however, a small farming community sprang up around it, the first time the Mongols ever attempted to grow their own grains and vegetables.

Genghis Khan's son Ogodei established the Mongol city Karakorum on the Orkhon River.

embrace their wives and daughters."[25] So much for moderation.

Yet, Genghis was not an unthinking man. He knew he could not rule the vast empire he had created in the same rapacious way he had conducted himself as a steppe warlord. Many of his biliks resonate with a philosophy that could almost be called humanistic. Historian Rene Grossett sums up his dilemma:

The paradox . . . lies in the contrast between the wise, reflective, and moral character of a leader who regulated his own conduct and that of his people by maxims of sound common sense and well-established justice and the brutal reactions of a people newly emerged from primitive savagery, who sought no other means than those of terror for the subjugation of their enemies—a people for whom human life had no value whatsoever and who, as nomads, lacked all conception of the life of sedentary peoples, of urban conditions or farming culture, or of anything alien to their native steppe.[26]

In the end, Genghis adopted a policy that combined both these tendencies. A subject people was given an ultimatum: total submission or total annihilation. Those who resisted were put to the sword. Those who chose to accept Mongol rule escaped with their lives, but they paid a cruel price. Their sons and daughters were enslaved, their possessions were plundered, and they were left to till the soil for the benefit of the Mongols who reappeared at will to take everything but the bare essentials of survival.

Advise and Consent

Genghis made all the decisions, but his court was not a one-man show. In fact, he was surrounded by a bureaucracy and household staff that would be the envy of the most self-aggrandizing potentate. His ten thousand-man personal guard, or keshig, doubled as household staff during rare moments of peace. They tended his herds, fetched his food, sharpened his weapons. They also guarded the life and safety of the Khan and his family, much like the Secret Service guards the president in America today. They patrolled his tents, beating intruders with sticks and shooting those who tried to flee with untipped arrows, a painful but not deadly punishment.

This select group was the elite of the Mongol Empire, enjoying privileges that exceeded even those of even military regimental commanders. From their ranks, Genghis chose the upper stratum of his advisers and imperial administrators. The group originally consisted of friends, andas, and nokod, but as it grew from one hundred to ten thousand it came to incorporate the sons of military commanders and many young men from conquered tribes. These were held as virtual hostages until they proved their loyalty to Genghis's satisfaction. Then, they were accorded his complete trust. On the surface, this seems to be a risky system, but there is no record that it ever failed and it is ranked as one of Genghis's great achievements.

The imperial guard was Genghis's innovation, but he borrowed the rest of his administrative framework from his enemies, notably the Khitans and the Uigurs, whose alphabet gave the Mongols a written language for the first time in their history. Because Genghis and his Mongol commanders and administrative officials were illiterate, scribes were essential to the conduct of imperial business and became an integral part of court life. In shifts, they sat by Genghis's side, faithfully recording his biliks and the more formal pronouncements that composed the Yasa.

The scribes also recorded letters to foreign rulers, usually demands for tribute and submission, accompanied by threats of annihilation for noncompliance. A team of translators then went to work and the letters were dispatched by courier to their destinations. Eventually, this ad hoc assembly of scribes and translators grew into an imperial secretariat, responsible for the maintenance of all records, including those pertaining to taxation and the census. Genghis appointed a member of the conquered Naiman tribe to be Keeper of the Seal, which was used to establish the authenticity of all official documents.

This secretariat came to have great influence. Because they were literate and grasped the intricacies of a money economy, something beyond the ken of the Mongols, who measured wealth in wives and horses, members of the secretariat had ample opportunity to abuse their position. Many did, and many paid with their lives when the wily Khan uncovered their fraud.

Basaqs and Daraugachi

Proven members of the guard were promoted to key positions in the administration of conquered lands, responsible for maintaining order and collecting taxes. This group consisted of basaqs and daraugachis. The basaqs were the Khan's agents in foreign territories, living among the conquered peoples and enforcing their authority with as many soldiers as they needed to carry out their duties.

They familiarized themselves with the local customs and power structure and journeyed back to the court to advise the Khan on how best to exploit the situation. These briefings were of vital importance because they ensured that tribute and tax revenue kept flowing into the royal coffers and that there was a steady supply of conscripts for the army.

As the empire grew, the basaq system became unwieldy. To maintain centralized control, Genghis appointed a new level of bureaucrat, the daraugachi. Unlike the basaqs, daraugachis lived permanently at court and each had a territory to oversee. The basaqs reported to them. Together they conducted an exact census of conquered peoples on which both taxes and conscription were based. The census was a serious affair— the economy of the empire depended on it—but they conducted at least one aspect of it in a typically Mongol way. If a given population rebelled and was massacred, the ears of the dead were collected and brought to court in sacks so the tax base could be recalculated.

The basaqs and the daraugachis collected three types of taxes. The first was tribute, called alba, a form of extortion that the conquered paid to the conqueror to avoid extermination. Like all "protection money," payment brought only a temporary respite from the threat of destruction. Whenever the basaqs determined that the local economy could survive another levy, more tribute was demanded on pain of death.

The second tax was less arbitrary. Called the qubchur, it was an annual 1 percent levy paid by everyone, including the nomads themselves, and it was used to support the court and the armies. The qubchur was always taken in livestock; the alba embraced anything the Mongols considered to be of value. The third tax, the 5 percent tamgha, was collected on all commercial transactions, both in goods and in services. The Mongols were quick to realize that the east-west trade routes they controlled were a valuable source of revenue.

Conquered people who rebelled lost their lives and their ears.

Spies and Scholars

Genghis Khan's traveling court became a rich melting pot of many cultures. He realized that the Mongols were not equipped to deal with the complexities of running an empire as vast as the one he was building and needed the administrative expertise of foreigners. Also, the Mongols came to envy the beauty and luxury of the artifacts and textiles they claimed as booty and tribute. Gold cups and bowls and silk and brocade clothing were particular favorites. Lacking the craftsmanship to make these things themselves, they enslaved goldsmiths, weavers, and other artisans.

Physicians, especially Persians, became court favorites after one of them cured Genghis of an eye infection that his shaman had failed to heal with incantations. Despite minor medical failings, the shamans remained powerful and ubiquitous figures at the court of the superstitious Khan, who called upon them repeatedly to verify that his heavenly mandate to rule the world was still in force and relied upon their prayers and prognostications before making all major, and many minor, decisions.

Genghis's interest in foreign cultures was more than material. He was an intensely curious man and liked to probe the minds of those whose scope and experience exceeded the limitations of the steppe. As always, he had a practical ulterior motive. The more he understood about foreign cultures, the better he would be able to exploit them for his own gain. Yet he regarded the astronomers, astrologers, scholars, scribes, and religious adepts whom he invited to his court as more than pawns in his deadly chess game of conquest.

Some of them even became his friends. He summoned a renowned Taoist monk, Chungchen, because he believed the elderly ascetic had discovered the secret of eternal life. The monk quickly shattered his illusion and then went on to browbeat him for his brutality and even for killing animals during the hunt. To a Mongol, these admonishments could have been nothing less than a total condemnation of his way of life and his very identity as a human being. Thousands had been summarily executed for less drastic offenses, but Genghis thanked the monk for sharing his wisdom and sent him on his way with a party of soldiers to guarantee his safe passage home. He continued to write to this man, who inhabited a cultural and spiritual universe so different from his own, and some years later dictated this touching letter to his friend: "Since you left me, Holy Eternal One, not a day has passed that I have not thought of you. Holy Eternal One, you must not forget me either."[27]

Courtiers and Visitors

Another fixture of the court were the dark-hans, men who had impressed the Khan with their bravery, loyalty, military prowess, or administrative brilliance. In contrast to many other members of his entourage, darkhans were usually Mongols, or at least from steppe tribes closely enough associated with the Mongols to fit comfortably under the name. The darkhans were the lords of the court. They were assigned titles like Cup Bearer and Quiver Bearer, after functions they performed on ceremonial occasions.

They had personal access to the Khan and were allowed to keep all the herds and booty they took in raids without having to share the wealth as those of lower rank were required to do. They also enjoyed exemptions from some of the laws that governed Mongol life. In keeping with Genghis's plan to break up

In return for protection, merchants often presented Genghis Khan with lavish gifts such as this gold buckle.

the power of tribe and clan, darkhans were chosen on the basis of their character and not on the basis of familial or tribal affiliation.

The ranks of the court were also swelled by merchants, lured by greed to embrace the protection the Mongols offered and always ready to curry favor with the upper echelon by presenting them with lavish gifts, gold artifacts and brocade clothing being the most likely to put a sparkle in Genghis's eyes.

Genghis prided himself on his frank and familiar manner in his dealings with other Mongols, insisting that business be conducted literally on a first-name basis. Foreigners, on the other hand, were put through a ritualistic dance of diplomatic etiquette lest they forget they were in the presence of an emperor who had been stamped with a heavenly seal of approval.

Foreign visitors to the court of the Great Khan had to observe a very precise protocol, breaches of which could have sudden and fatal consequences. When they approached the nine-pointed white standard that flew proudly outside his ger, they had to bow three times and could be ushered in only by a member of the household guard. The price of admission, so to speak, was a gift of gold, silver, pearls, damask, or brocade. A handsome hunting falcon or sable vest would do in a pinch.

Without some such token of esteem, the hoped-for meeting would likely not take place at all or end in a summary beheading if the Khan did not quickly perceive some advantage in keeping the hapless transgressor alive. The interview was conducted through translators, with the supplicant on his knees with his head humbly bowed. The Khan sat austerely and silently while the supplication was made, then settled the issue with a nod or a shake of his head. If all went well, the foreigner was sent home with a standard message, a kind of imperial form letter, for his leader. This letter, embodying the disdain with which the Mongols regarded the rest of the world, matter-of-factly demanded total submission to the Khan's rule and praised the foreign potentate in advance for his wisdom in accepting Genghis's authority.

No letter dictated by Genghis himself has survived, but scholars believe one dispatched from his grandson Guyuk to Pope Innocent

IV retains the haughty tone of the originals: "This command is sent to the Great Pope. . . . Your request to submit and to be subservient to Us, sent to Us through Your ambassadors, has been examined. If You wish to act according to Your own words then You, Great Pope, together with all the Kings, must come here in person and do homage to Us."[28]

World Dominance

Genghis Khan's transformation of steppe society through his reforms enabled the Mongols, who originally numbered about seven hundred thousand, to rule an empire of 100 million people. The reforms enabled him to maintain a strong central government while preserving the nomadic mobility and tribal loyalties that made the Mongols strong.

By reining in the power of clan and tribal chiefs, he was able to focus the aggressiveness that tribal warfare inspired outward on the wealthy civilizations that surrounded the steppe. In so doing he not only preserved the Mongols from self-destruction but gave them the basis for world domination.

Genghis's "activities were not limited to military field," says his biographer Paul Ratchnevsky. "His successes owed less to his military skills than to his astute policies and organizational abilities. The empire he built outlived him by more than a century."[29]

The Mongol War Machine

The reforms that Genghis Khan instituted in Mongol society were a means to an end and not an end in themselves. His goal was to create an army so powerful that no force it encountered could stand in its way. By basing his reorganization on the system of tens, he effectively mobilized the entire nation for war. Since the leaders of the arbans, jaghuns, and minghans were also military officers, every Mongol man, woman, and child was a member of a disciplined military machine and each had a role to play in their emperor's military campaigns.

The hundreds of thousands who fell victim to the Mongol sword during Genghis's reign are silent witnesses to the magnitude of his success and his reputation as history's most ruthless master of the art of warfare.

"The history of the Mongol armies is a catalogue of superlatives," writes military historian S. R. Turnbull:

No armies in history have ever won so many battles or conquered so much territory. No army has ever provoked such justifiable terror and loathing in its victims, or slaughtered so many of its vanquished. . . . What other army in history has

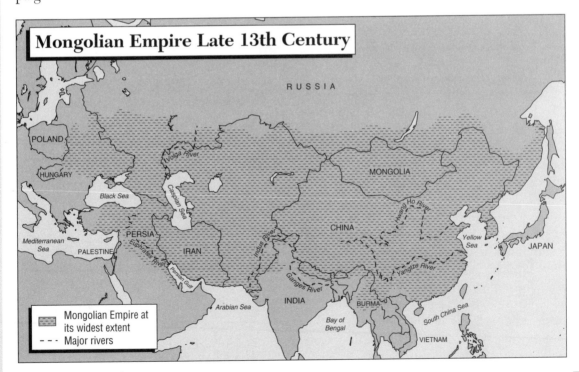

Mongolian Empire Late 13th Century

RUSSIA

POLAND

HUNGARY

Volga River

Black Sea

Caspian Sea

Mediterranean Sea

PALESTINE

PERSIA

Euphrates River

IRAN

Persian Gulf

Indus River

Arabian Sea

Ganges River

INDIA

Bay of Bengal

BURMA

VIETNAM

MONGOLIA

Hwang Ho River

CHINA

Yangtze River

Yellow Sea

JAPAN

South China Sea

Mongolian Empire at its widest extent
- - - Major rivers

marched on Russia in winter and survived, let alone won victories? What other army, indeed, could have attacked Russia in winter by choice [alluding to the defeats suffered by Napoléon and Adolf Hitler's armies in similar undertakings] because the frozen rivers and deep snow made communication easier?

These are the achievements that have made the Mongols the object of admiration and loathing ever since they erupted on to the world scene in 1206 when Genghis Khan, "under the command and guidance of heaven," set out to conquer the world. It was a world far wider than that subdued by the great Alexander, who, we are told, wept because he had no world left to conquer. By the end of the 13th century Mongol armies had been in action in countries as far apart as Poland, Japan, Hungary, Russia, Palestine, Persia, India, Burma and Vietnam. Teutonic knights of Germany and samurai of Japan, while ignorant of each other's existence, had in fact fought a common enemy.[31]

The Mongol Warrior

The backbone of Genghis Khan's army was the Mongol soldier himself, a humble herdsman during rare moments of peace, but a savage warrior in the frequent times of strife. In non-nomadic societies, armies had to be raised from farming populations, unfamiliar with weaponry, and journeymen horse riders at best. They were also unused to discipline and wanted to return home to their families far more than they wanted to fight the enemy.

The Mongols, on the other hand, had been riding—living in the saddle, in fact—and shooting bows and arrows since they were toddlers. The migrations and hunts had incul-

cated principles of discipline that equipped them naturally for the battlefield. Their families and herds, in the nomadic tradition, traveled with them. Also, life on the steppe required that they have their own horses and weapons, so Genghis did not have the monumental problem of outfitting them, a crippling burden on the economies of his adversaries.

The Mongol cavalry soldier was self-sufficient. He traveled with three or four horses—more if he could afford them—which he rode in rotation. This enabled the armies to cover vast amounts of territory quickly. "On a campaign," Turnbull says, "his speed was . . . increased by always taking with him between one and four remounts, which were ridden in turn for periods of up to 24 hours."[31] His herds and wife, or wives, were nearby to satisfy his need for food and clothing.

Although women normally played a supporting role during military operations, they were adept riders and archers and joined their husbands in battle if their participation made the difference between victory and defeat. Children were put to work repairing armor and helping their mothers support their fathers as soon as they were old enough to do so.

Armor

A soldier's armor and weaponry depended on his wealth, and records indicate that the poorest among them often went into battle with nothing but bow and arrow. That was rare. Most wore an effective, lightweight suit of armor made from layered panels of leather stitched together by animal sinews. This type of body armor, called lamellar, was not a Mongol invention. It had a long history in Asian warfare and a similar type of armor was worn by the samurai warriors of Japan.

The leather was treated with pitch to

make it waterproof and to increase its resistance to enemy arrows and sword blades, but the principal advantage of lamellar armor is its lightness and flexibility, crucial considerations for a mounted soldier involved in the fast-paced action that Mongol tactics required. A medieval European knight, by contrast, had severely limited motion and mobility due to the weight of his massively heavy metal suit of armor.

The Mongol soldier was protected by a lamellar breastplate and often a backplate as well. In addition, he wore a sleeveless knee-length lamellar coat, fastened only at the waist so it wouldn't interfere with his ability to ride his horse. In some instances, he wore similar leather plates on his arm and legs. On his feet he wore leather boots over thick felt socks, and a metal helmet with leather flaps protected his head, the back of his neck, and the sides of his face. In winter, he wore a fur overcoat, sometimes two. In the latter case, the fur side of one coat would be turned toward his skin and that of the other outward.

His underwear was made of wool or fleece or, if he could afford it, silk. The Chinese had discovered the military advantages of silk undergarments and the Mongols quickly borrowed the innovation. If a soldier was struck by an arrow, the surprisingly tough silk fabric would wrap itself around the arrowhead, making it possible to remove it from his flesh with a minimum of tissue damage.

Weapons and Other Gear

Each soldier carried two bows and three quivers containing thirty arrows each. He used two types of arrows: lighter ones with highly sharpened points to shoot over long distances and heavier ones with broad heads for fighting at close quarters. Friar Carpini observed that

The Mongol warrior was well equipped to withstand the rigors of long military campaigns.

both types of arrows were "tempered when they are hot in water mixed with salt . . . so that they should be strong for penetrating armor."[32]

The Mongol warrior also carried a curved, single-edged saber, a lance with hook for pulling opponents from their saddles, a battle ax, a knife, and occasionally a javelin and a heavy club. In addition, his kit included a small cooking pot, an awl and sinews for repairing his armor, a file or rasp to sharpen his weapons, fishing line, a horsehair lasso, and two leather bottles. This gear was carried in waterproof saddlebags that could be inflated to help the soldier ford rivers.

His horse wore lamellar armor similar to

The Mongol Bow

The Mongol bow is a prime example of the use of primitive materials to their best and most efficient advantage. It was of composite construction, made from layers of horn and hardened animal sinews on a wooden frame, to give it enhanced strength. Each soldier carried two, the larger of which had a draw weight (a measure of the amount of strength required to pull the bow string) of 166 pounds. It is vivid testimony to the muscular strength of the Mongol archer—modern competition bows have a draw weight of about 50 pounds. It had a range of 300 yards, far greater than the longbow used in Europe during the same period. Only the invention of the gun gave soldiers a weapon with a greater range and more rapid rate of fire.

his own and grazed and drank water on the move. His wooden saddle weighed about ten pounds and curved up at both the front and rear to provide a stable seat during battle. It was covered with skins and pelts to provide a small measure of comfort. His iron stirrups were suspended from the saddle with short straps, enabling him to stand while using his bow and arrow or wielding his saber. If he was on sentry duty, he carried a shield made of wicker or leather, but he did not use a shield in battle.

Each unit of ten men had a small ger, which was carried on the back of a pack horse. They also brought their hunting gear with them—they used different sorts of arrows when hunting than they did in battle—and this, too, was transported on the pack horses. Larger units often brought battering rams, catapults, and other siege weapons if their goal was to capture an entire city.

Rations

The Mongol soldier lived on meager rations: some dried meat, a little dried milk to be mixed with water, and of course, kumiss to warm his spirit during long winter rides and bolster his courage in battle. European adventurer and famed chronicler Marco Polo marveled at how little food the soldiers ate without appearing to suffer any loss of strength and stamina: "Often enough, if need be, they will go or stay for a whole month without provisions, drinking only the milk of a mare and eating wild game of their own taking."[33]

Genghis insisted that when food was scarce all the fighting men share equally in what was available without distinction of rank. Officers as well as ordinary soldiers had to make do with whatever was available. They had no scruples about eating things that appalled the more refined taste of a European observer like Carpini. "They regard anything which can be eaten as food," the shocked friar wrote. "They eat dogs, wolves, foxes and horses."[34]

The only horses they would eat were those killed in battle or so badly wounded as to destroy their military usefulness. But they did perfect a technique, used only in times of extreme privation, whereby they could subsist by drinking a horse's blood, which they obtained by piercing a vein in the animal's neck, drinking a small amount, then stitching the wound. In this way, both horse and rider were able to survive the harshest conditions.

Their horses too were battle toughened. Polo reports that the hardy animals were able to "support themselves by grazing," relieving the army of the burden of transporting fodder for them. Together, horse and rider made a formidable fighting team. "They will stay all night on horseback under arms, while their mount goes on steadily cropping the grass." Polo continues, "They are of all the men in the world the best able to endure exertion and hardship and the least costly to maintain and therefore the best adapted for conquering territory and overthrowing kingdoms."[35]

Discipline

The Mongol army was nothing less than the entire population mobilized for war. Fighting was just another part of life, like hunting and herding, for which they had been conditioned from youth. The army was indistinguishable from the rest of society. When Genghis Khan went to war, the entire Mongol nation went with him. This cre-

ated a monumental discipline problem, but once again Genghis was equal to the challenge.

He extended the decimal system of arbans, jaguns and minghans to include tumens, each comprising ten minghans. These ten thousand-man tumens were further combined in groups of two or three to compose armies. Genghis usually had several armies in the field at any given time, often fighting wars on different fronts. Each army was led by a general and each of the lesser groupings by commanders ranked in descending order of importance.

As an inducement to obedience and self-sacrifice, Genghis instituted a system of collective responsibility that was rigorously enforced by his commanders. Carpini described the system in this way:

By stalking their enemy and silently surrounding them, Mongol warriors were able to carry out surprise attacks.

When the line goes into battle, if one or two or three or more flee from the squad of ten, all ten are killed; and if all ten flee, unless the rest of the hundred flee, all of them are killed. Briefly, unless they all give way together, all who flee are killed. Also, if one or two or more proceed daringly into the fight and the remainder of the ten do not follow, they are killed; and if one or more of the ten is captured and the other comrades do not free them, again they are killed.[36]

To ensure the loyalty of his commanders, Genghis exacted an oath of allegiance and demanded that they forfeit a son or younger brother to his guard and household staff, where they were held as virtual hostages. Early in his career, his lieutenants swore the following oath, entitling him to take all they had, including their wives and children, should they fail to follow his orders in either war or peace: "If we, a day of battle, violate thine orders, severing us from our goods, from our ladies and wives, go thou, forsaking on the earth and ground our black heads. If we, a day of peace, break thy counsel, severing us from household and goods, from our wives and children, go thou, forsaking us in a land without a lord."[37]

The Mongol Blitzkrieg

The frightful term *blitzkrieg*, coined by the Nazis at the outset of World War II to describe the lightning swiftness of the German army (*"blitz"* means lightning and *"krieg"* means war), could have been conceived with the Mongols in mind. Their tactics were devised to take advantage of the incredible speed of their armed warriors. That speed was truly impressive—the Mongol army could cover about three times the distance of any contemporary adversary army in the same amount of time. In 1221, Genghis led his cav-

Because the entire Mongol population participated in the army, fighting was simply a way of life.

Mongol Cruelty: Pros and Cons

Much has been made of the barbarity of the Mongol army. Stories abound of enemies being boiled alive, cannibalized, or sewn into blankets and trampled to death by horses. One account even maintains that Genghis himself ordered one foe executed by having molten silver poured into his eyes. The cannibalism and the molten silver episode appear to be fabrications, bred by the terror the Mongols inspired in their enemies, but boiling and trampling as methods of execution do have a basis in fact. The Mongols believed that to kill a valiant adversary by spilling his blood would release his revenge-bent spirit into the world. They didn't hesitate to cut off the heads of lesser mortals—whose weaker spirits posed only a minor threat—but when confronted with a respected foe, they turned to other methods of execution. The boiling of enemies was a tradition the Mongols inherited from their Siberian neighbors; while there is no evidence that Genghis Khan ever resorted to this practice, his anda Jamuka certainly did. Make no mistake, the Mongols were ruthless and brutal in battle, often using their enemies to fill moats and ditches so their horses and pack animals could cross and also using them as cannon fodder in the front lines of attacks. While they killed willingly, they apparently did it quickly when circumstances permitted and didn't torture people for their own amusement.

alry 130 miles in just two days. Even more astounding, one of his most trusted generals, Subedei, led an entire army 180 miles in three days through deep snow to attack Russia in 1241.

The army stalked enemies like hunters pursued game, silently and resolutely encircling at a steady and relentless trot, then announcing the moment of the kill with terrifying shrieks as they unleashed a lethal rain of arrows and broke into a gallop. Scouts had previously reconnoitered the terrain thoroughly, so the main army knew to close off all escape routes. The feigned retreat was a favorite tactic. Marco Polo describes it thus:

They are never ashamed to have recourse to flight. They maneuver freely, shooting at the enemy, now from this quarter, now from that. They have trained their horses so well that they wheel this way or that as quickly as a dog would do. When they are pursued and take to flight, they fight as well and as effectively as when they are face to face with the enemy. When they are fleeing at top speed, they twist around with their bows and let fly their arrows to such good purpose that they kill the horses of the enemy and the riders too. When the enemy thinks he has routed and crushed them, then he is lost; for he finds his horses killed and not a few of his men. As soon as the Tartars [that's what the Europeans called all the people of the steppe] decide that they have killed enough of the pursuing horses and horsemen, they wheel around and attack and acquit themselves so well and so courageously that they gain a complete victory.[38]

Genghis also used spies and psychological warfare to further his ends, in both case employing merchants to carry out his orders. In exchange for Mongol protection, traders would report back to the Khan's court on the economic, political, and military strengths and weakness of target territories. They would also disseminate false information about the Mongols' activities and troop movements and spread tales of the brutality with which they treated all people who refused to submit meekly to them.

Using spies, Genghis Khan passed false information about his troops' movements in order to defeat his enemies.

In 1228, Genghis sent a caravan of 450 merchants to the Islamic city of Utrar, near the Aral Sea. "The governor of the city, asserting, no doubt correctly, that these so-called merchants were in fact spies, had them all killed and their property confiscated," writes David Morgan. Genghis sent ambassadors to protest. When they, too, were killed, he unleashed a campaign that Morgan describes as "the greatest calamity ever to befall the people of the eastern Islamic world."[39]

Rewarding the Mongol Warrior

Much was demanded of the Mongol soldier, but much was offered in return. Genghis insisted that commanders treat their troops fairly and humanely. Both officers and men ate the same rations and all shared in the booty that frequently was the sole point of the raids. Military glory in Genghis's army was the way for an ordinary Mongol to increase his wealth and prestige and to overcome the handicaps of his birth by adding livestock to his herds.

It also made it possible for women who distinguished themselves in battle to accumulate wealth and social standing that was not dependent on that of a husband. "For men, and sometimes women, war was the key to prestige and honor," says David Christian. "While successful management of one's herds ensured bare survival, and fortunate marriages created useful connections, success in battle promised wealth, status and power."[40]

Those who committed acts of great bravery were often rewarded by being named darkhans and admitted to Genghis's inner circle of advisers and court favorites. For example, two humble herdsmen named Badai and

Kishlik risked their lives to save Genghis from capture during one of his early campaigns on the steppe. The Khan raised them and their children and grandchildren to the status of darkhans, granting them the right to retain all the spoils they took in battle and all the animals they killed during the hunt without having to share with the other members of their tribe.

Coupled with grievous punishment for disobedience, this lavish system of reward worked effectively to ensure the discipline required to transform a nation of herders into the greatest army the world has ever seen.

Husbands, Wives, and Children

The Mongol family was efficiently organized to meet the rigorous demands imposed by the harsh economic realities of their nomadic existence. Everyone had to pitch in daily to guarantee the necessities of life. From the earliest age possible both boys and girls learned the necessary skills of successful nomads. As adults, even into old age, men and women shared equally in the physically punishing—and dangerous—labor required by herding and hunting.

This equality was reinforced during Genghis Khan's military campaigns. If the men were occupied with fighting, the women, children, and able-bodied elderly had to shoulder all the responsibilities the menfolk normally performed during peacetime. The result was a remarkably homogenous family unit. Children assumed adult responsibilities much sooner than they did in non-nomadic societies and women enjoyed far greater influence in the decisions that affected family life than did their agrarian counterparts.

In fact, European and Arabic observers of the Mongols were all surprised, and impressed, by the relatively high status women enjoyed among the peoples of the steppe compared with what they were used to back home. They also heaped praise on the physical toughness and fortitude of both women and children.

But they were ominously silent on the subject of the elderly, beyond a few oblique comments that the Mongols did not treat them well. This has given rise to the belief that old people were cast aside when they had outlived their economic and military usefulness, a harsh and unfair assessment. Because the Mongols were especially hardy, these outside observers often failed to note that men were routinely conscripted into the army until the age of seventy! The demanding life of the steppe ensured that Mongols remained strong and vigorous well past the age when more "civilized" people took to the medieval equivalent of the rocking chair.

Even in old age, Mongolians remained vigorous and productive members of the community.

The Homestead

Talk of a nomadic family's homestead may sound like a contradiction in terms, but Mongol life centered around the ger—the mobile felt tent—which was both a home and a homestead even though it moved constantly with the migrating herds and the army. The ger was an effective shelter from the elements, but it was much, much more. It was where the Mongols lived, loved, raised their children, and worshiped their gods.

The structure and orientation of the ger was dictated by religious considerations. The fire of dried dung that the women carefully built in the precise center of the tent was more than a warming hearth and cooking pit. It also represented the center of the spiritual universe and the smoke that rose from it through the skylight symbolized a passageway, rising upward to link the earthbound Mongols of this world with the spirit realm.

The door of every ger always faced south, not only to shield those inside from the cold north wind, but because south is the direction toward which the Mongols faced when they prayed, in much the same way the Muslims pray facing Mecca. The west is associated with the male principle of life, the east with the female. Therefore, given the south-facing direction of the ger, men occupied the right side of the tent and women the left.

Every ger contained a shrine where the family kept felt idols of nature spirits and ancestors. The women made and maintained these idols and both men and women made sacrifices of milk, blood, animal fat, or kumiss (the Mongols' favorite alcoholic beverage) to them every morning and prior to every important undertaking, especially hunts, migrations, and battles.

The permanent skylight of the ger symbolized a spiritual passageway linking those on earth with the spirit realm.

Special felt idols bracketed the ger's doorway. These represented the gods of happiness and good fortune and gave rise to a Mongol custom that cost many unwitting foreign visitors their lives. Stepping on the tent flap of a ger was such a profound insult to these gods and the family they protected that offenders were summarily put to death. Another idol, fashioned from felt and rags in the shape of an udder, was proudly displayed and worshiped in every ger. Sheep were often sacrificed to it to ensure the health of the flocks and herds and a plentiful supply of milk.

Adults and older children slept on the felt-lined floor of the ger in their clothes, covered by animal pelts in winter. Infants were afforded the comfort of cradles, carefully carved by their fathers. A family with the

The elaborately decorated door of the ger faced south, the direction in which the mongols prayed.

means to do so would adorn the cradle with jewels and gold captured as booty or exacted as tribute from conquered peoples. For a people not renowned for their hygiene, the Mongols kept their gers scrupulously clean. It is testimony to the uninhibited lives they led that there was a universally recognized prohibition against urinating inside someone's ger. If the offense was deemed to be accidental, a heavy fine was imposed. However, if it was a willful act, the punishment was beheading.

A wealthy Mongol might have several gers, one for each of his wives and their children. If that was the case, they were arranged to the east in descending order of wifely importance, with the first or chief wife inhabiting the tent closest to that of the patriarch. Other gers might be set aside for slaves, if the family had any, and vassals in case the patriarch was a powerful warlord chief. Herds and flocks were kept nearby as were carts, weapons, and supplies.

Child Labor

Mongol children had to grow up quickly—there was much work to be done and they had to do their share. By the time they were two or three years old, both boys and girls had started their training in horsemanship. Taught by their fathers and uncles, they took their first rides on lambs, graduating to sheep and ponies as soon as they were big enough to handle larger animals. At the age of nine or ten, they were as comfortable in the saddle of a full-size horse as they were on foot.

As they honed their riding skills, they were taught to shoot with tiny bows and arrows, specially crafted to suit their small hands and arm spans. This early military training was mandatory for both sexes. They polished their aim by shooting first at birds and then at small game like rabbits and foxes. The animals they killed were a source of food, making them a productive part of the family economy while they were still learning the skills essential to survival on the steppe.

The goal was to make every Mongol boy a potential soldier, both to protect and increase the family's herds by engaging in battle with rival tribes, and to be ready when the Khan called on them to join his military campaigns. But girls also learned the arts of war. If the family or clan was attacked, they were expected to be able to defend themselves. They were exempt from the universal conscription to which boys were subject from the age of fifteen on, but Friar Carpini notes: "Girls and women ride and gallop on horses as skillfully as the men. We even saw them carrying quivers and bows. . . . All of them, from the children to the adults are good archers."[44]

Both boys and girls were carefully taught the techniques of herding and milking and other aspects of animal husbandry. They were expected to stand guard duty and ride with the adults during the seasonal migrations. At this point a small division of labor does begin to creep into the picture. Boys learned how to make and repair weapons— bows, arrows, lances, swords. Girls were taught by their mothers and older sisters— and their father's other wives—how to cook and make clothes from leather and felt and to repair the gers.

With all that work, there was little time for play. The few mentions of childhood recreation that occur in original sources refer to a game resembling jacks that youngsters played with bone chips and a hockeylike pastime played on frozen ponds during the long winters, in which a sheep's shank bone was used instead of a puck. Pets were almost unknown. Dogs were ferocious creatures trained to guard the camp and herds and the Mongols did not keep domesticated cats. Privileged children were sometimes allowed to keep birds, but more likely were encouraged to use them for target practice rather than as companions.

From an early age, both Mongol boys and girls were taught the techniques of herding and milking cattle.

Women as Warriors and Workers

Women played an important yet ambiguous role in the Mongol family. In certain respects, they were treated like chattel, captured in battle and divided among the soldiers like livestock and other spoils of war. Yet they wielded considerable power and enjoyed a social status superior to that of women in farming civilizations. From childhood, they were trained to do everything men could do.

As adults, they were expected to take over all male functions when the men were at war or participating in the annual hunt. Their riding skills equaled those of men and in some instances they proved to be formidable fighters with both bow and sword. David Christian notes that Mongols were hardly feminists by today's standards, but points out that they necessarily had to overcome traditional gender stereotypes: "Inequalities of gender have also existed in pastoralist societies, but they seem to have been softened by the absence of steep hierarchies of wealth in most communities, and also by the requirement that women acquire most of the skills of men, including, often, their military skills."[42]

What the Mongols Ate

The Mongol diet would horrify a modern cardiologist: The Mongols lived almost exclusively on meat and dairy products. There is no mention of bread or vegetables in the contemporary accounts of their lives and the only grain they ate was millet, which they boiled into a gruel for their morning meal. Nor did they use cooking oil of any kind. Horsemeat, mutton, and game were either roasted or boiled and eaten by hand from small bowls. They also drank the boiling liquid as a broth and made dried sausages and jerky to eat on the move.

The staple of their unusual diet was mare's milk. They drank it straight or dried it to take with them on journeys. They also made various kinds of cheeses. They obtained most of their meat by hunting or from animals that died naturally, preferring not to deplete their herds by slaughtering their livestock. In winter, they preserved meat by burying it in the frozen ground.

Waste of any kind was punished severely and they ate virtually every part of an animal except the fecal matter and urine found in its intestines and bladder. They didn't even toss bones to the camp dogs without first extracting and eating the marrow. They drank water sparingly because they believed it to be sacred. When they had to, they fasted. Two days without food didn't seem to slow them down at all, even in battle, and they were said to have been able to carry on for ten days if no food was available.

Reports that they engaged in cannibalism appear to be exaggerated, but they did eat dogs, wolves, foxes, and even the afterbirth of foaling mares if they had to. They also drank the blood of their horses to stave off dehydration during long marches by opening a vein in the horse's neck, drinking their fill, and closing it again with no harm to the animal.

Though food was often scarce, hospitality was a social obligation that was taken very seriously. A hungry traveler could approach any fire and eat without invitation, and refusal to extend hospitality was high on the list of social taboos.

Mongol women were often excellent warriors and had horse-riding skills that equaled their male counterparts.

Although the society was structured on patriarchal lines, men willingly sought and listened to women's opinions. Even the young Genghis Khan was subject to criticism for paying too much attention to his first wife, Borte, who urged him to break with his blood brother Jamuka and with his steppe lord Togril. Mongol women could be relentless in pursuit of their goals. When Jamuka had accepted that Genghis was about to execute him as as traitor, he gave an impassioned speech outlining the reasons why his life was no longer worth living, citing his babbling, shrewish wife high on the list.

Mongol women could inherit property from their husbands. When a chief died, his first wife took over the reins of power until the succession was settled. Her decisions in this vital matter were heavily weighed, even at the lofty level of who would run the empire following the death of Genghis Khan's successor Ogodei. Because the custom of marital exogamy dictated that they come from other tribes, women also had great influence in establishing tribal alliances. Frequently, a wife's kinfolk became the allies of her husband and her traditional enemies became his as well.

At a more day-to-day level, women were responsible for rearing children, a task they shared among them in multiwife families. They were responsible for making clothes; repairing the ger, which they did with thread made from animal sinews; and cooking the food. They also loaded and unloaded the carts, a backbreaking chore which sometimes included hoisting the entire tent and all its contents. Men, by contrast, spent their time making and mending weapons, saddles, saddlebags, and wooden carts and amusing themselves with hunting and war games.

Beyond this minimal division of labor, all other tasks were a joint responsibility and women needed as much strength and stamina as men to carry them out. Except on ceremonial occasions, and at the Khan's court, men and women dressed alike, leading foreign observers to complain of the difficulty of telling them apart.

Friar Carpini was impressed by the industry of the hardworking Mongol women he observed: "The Tatar [his mistaken name for the Mongols] women make everything: skin clothes, shoes, leggings, and everything made of leather. They drive carts and repair them, they load camels, and are quick and vigorous in all their tasks."[43]

Marriage

A Mongol man could have many wives, but he married only once. His first wife, who was chosen for him by his parents before he was a teenager, was the only one sanctioned by customary steppe law. His other wives were usually taken forcibly in battle or given to him as tribute by a clan or tribe he had vanquished. In arranged marriages, it was usual for the wife to be somewhat older than her husband so that he could benefit from her superior wisdom and more extensive experience.

The groom's family and that of the bride subjected each other to careful scrutiny. The bride's parents demanded an accounting of the number of horses and other animals the groom would be likely to inherit. The Mongol husband was expected to be a good provider and a wife could demand a divorce if he failed to live up to expectations.

The groom's family was concerned about the bride's character, temperament, and physical hardiness. Would she fit in harmoniously with the extended family? Would she get along with her mother-in-law, who would ex-pect obedience? Would she be able to do the work demanded of her? Would she bear healthy children? Would she be able to share—without jealousy—her husband with the other wives he would, it was hoped, eventually acquire?

The families then turned to the shaman to consult the spirits to see if the marriage would be blessed. Prayers and sacrifices were offered and oracles consulted. If the omens were unfavorable, the marriage did not take place. No Mongol would tempt fate by taking such a big step without the approval of the gods and spirits. However, they were a practi-

While a Mongol marriage was arranged by family members, it was approved by the spirits.

cal people. If there was a strong political reason for the marriage to go forward, another shaman would be called in for what amounted to a spiritual second opinion. Bribes and less friendly inducements to arrive at a favorable conclusion were not unheard-of. The shamans, too, were pragmatists.

Once these considerations were settled, a protracted period of negotiation ensued over the bride-price, or dowry. Gift giving was an important part of the glue that held Mongol society together, and the gift that accompanied a bride was perhaps the most important of all. Borte's family gave Genghis Khan's father a luxurious sable coat, an impressive gift indeed, as sable clothing was held in high esteem by the Mongols as a symbol of status and respect.

The bride-price could also be paid in livestock, jewelry, or gold. Whatever form it took, families valued status in goods and would try to be as lavish as it could afford. After all, the alliance that was being forged could have wide-ranging consequences. Betrothal etiquette demanded reciprocity from the groom's family. In Genghis's case, it was determined that he would stay with Borte's clan to provide an extra hand to help with the herds. His stay was cut sharply short when his father was poisoned on his way home, but this arrangement could have lasted until the marriage was consummated six years later.

The age of majority for a Mongol man was fifteen; from then on he was an adult and that was the age at which most first marriages took place. The event was wildly celebrated with a feast and drinking party that often lasted for three days or more. To commemorate the event, and to mark herself as a married woman, the bride cut her hair very short and shaved the sides of her head, the Mongol equivalent of a wedding ring.

When he turned fifteen, Genghis decided to claim Borte as his bride, and traveled to her family to assert his rights. It is a ringing testimony to his forceful character that the wedding took place even though his fortunes were, at that time, at an ebb. Perhaps his in-laws saw in him the makings of the powerful steppe chief he would become. Yet, they were evidently concerned—Borte's mother accompanied the newlyweds back to Genghis's homestead to cast a stern maternal eye over the conditions in which her daughter would be living.

Borte quickly bore Genghis four sons, the future khans whose own sons would stretch the Mongol Empire to the limit of its expansion. Like all Mongol wives, she also tended the herds and the gers and, since her husband was perpetually at war, traveled with him on his campaigns. As the wife of an up-and-coming steppe chief, she was a particularly attractive target for his enemies, and paid the price when she was kidnapped and raped during a battle with a Merkit war party. Genghis Khan's "official" court biography, *The Secret History of the Mongols*, gives this dramatic episode short shrift. It appears that the man whose reputation for fierceness and bravery was to blaze so brightly ran away rather than leap to her defense. When he rescued her nine months later, he embraced her back into his life, even though she had been forced to live as another man's concubine and was pregnant with a child whose paternity would always be in doubt. Their reunion, as described in *The Secret History*, is touching. As the Merkit fled in fear, Genghis rode after them calling her name: "When he looked, recognizing Borte, they threw themselves upon each other in embracing each other. Then speaking that night he said, 'I have found my necessity which I sought.'"[44]

Wives and Concubines

Jealousy, it seems, played a minor role in the relationships between Mongol men and women, even though polygamous living arrangements gave it ample opportunity to rear its divisive head. Marco Polo could barely contain his astonishment at how smoothly things ran in the families he observed. "The wives are true and loyal to their husbands and very good at their household tasks," he wrote:

The European Marco Polo (pictured), who chronicled the lives of the Mongols in the 13th century, marveled at how smoothly their households ran.

Even if there as many as ten or twenty of them in one household, they live together in concord and unity beyond praise, so that you never hear a harsh word spoken. They all devote themselves to their various tasks and the care of the children, who are held among them in common. Their mode of marriage is such that any man may take as many wives as he pleases, even up to a hundred, if he is able to support them.[45]

Later in the same passage, Polo touches on another complicating aspect of Mongol married life, getting the general principles right, but making a mistake in one detail: "When a father dies, the eldest son marries the father's wives, excluding his own mother. He may also marry his brother's wife, if the brother dies."[46] Actually, according to the law and custom of the steppe, it was the youngest son who inherited his father's widows. Not mentioned by Polo, but nonetheless true, is the fact that women had the right to refuse to marry under these circumstances and choose to live as dowagers. Although Mongol men felt it was their right to have their way freely with women from unallied tribes, they scrupulously respected the wishes, even the whims, of women who were officially part of their own.

Virginity in women was valued only in the first wife; the others, whether inherited from dead relatives or captured in battle, had often been married before. If a woman had children, her new husband accepted them as his own. Although the first wife had special status in the Mongol family—she was always served first on ceremonial occasions, for example, and her ger, if there was more than one, was always to the immediate left of her husband's—she was frequently replaced by a succession of younger women, who for a time enjoyed the status of "favorite wife." Thus

Drinking

The Mongols liked to drink alcohol so much that they elevated the habit to the status of a national pastime. They grew neither grain nor grape, and so could not make wine, beer, or liquor, but they figured out a way to turn what they did have into an alcoholic beverage. Their drink of choice was called kumiss, fermented mare's milk. They churned the milk until they could extract the butter. The remaining liquid was high in lactose, the kind of sugar found in milk, which triggered the fermentation process. The result had quite a kick, according to European travelers who were compelled to join their hosts in marathon drinking sessions.

Their preference for kumiss notwithstanding, the Mongols would drink anything they could get their hands on, and wine was a popular booty item when they were raiding agricultural communities. In fact, when they overran the part of western Asia that is now Iran, they saw to it that the once-thriving wine industry, allowed to decline because of the Muslim prohibition against drinking, was quickly revived.

Mongol parties, which they held to celebrate weddings, successful raids, the annual hunt, the seasonal migrations, and any other notable occasion, were wild, boozy blowouts that lasted for days. Friar Carpini complained that they drank until they were sick and, once they recovered, picked up right where they left off. Women could hold their own with the men, and shocked Carpini with their raucous vulgarity when they were drunk. But he also noted that there was no sexual misbehavior at these Mongol shindigs, and very little fighting or even arguing.

The downside of excessive drinking is alcoholism and the Mongols fell victim to this vice. Stories abound about men who drank away their herds and were reduced to begging—even selling their children—to sustain themselves. The imperial family did not escape. Genghis Khan's youngest son Tolui drank himself to death at the age of forty, his grandson Kubai Khan followed suit after tiring of ruling China as founder of the Yuan dynasty, and even Ogodei, the son who succeeded him as Great Khan, had to be chastised for his excessive fondness for kumiss. Older brother Chaggadai was so concerned about Ogodei's drinking that he appointed a "minder" to limit him to one bowl of kumiss a day. Ogodei, demonstrating the ingenuity that was later to make him an effective Khan, responded by using a much larger bowl.

Genghis was fond of kumiss himself, but he was so alarmed by its harmful effects on his people that he tried to pass edicts to keep it under control. However, the man who conquered nations realized that in this area his powers were inadequate. Biographer Paul Ratchnevsky quotes Genghis: "If there is then no means to prevent drunkeness, a man may become drunk thrice a month; if he oversteps this limit he makes himself guilty of a punishable offence. If he is drunk twice a month, that is better—if only once, that is more praiseworthy. What could be better than that he should not drink at all? But where shall we find a man who never drinks? If, however, such a man is found, he deserves every respect."

Borte continued to command utmost respect even though Genghis was in the habit of bringing back a new wife from every military campaign until his collection of "trophy" spouses numbered by some accounts five hundred. These additional wives were status symbols, reflecting a man's financial ability to support them. They also provided labor and children who, as they grew up, added to the family workforce.

In practical terms, the man moved from wife to wife as the mood took him, usually spending most of his time with the favorite of the moment. Adultery was forbidden on pain of death, but this ban applied only to relations with women who were married to members of a man's tribe or clan and not to outsiders no matter what their marital status was. The point of the ban was not to uphold some moral precept, but promote social cohesion by eliminating a possible area of conflict in much the same way that robbery was punish-

able but plunder was a praiseworthy activity. Both bans were so effective that foreign visitors marveled at the chastity of the women and the absence of locks on doors and property chests.

Though the women were sexually beyond reproach, they were no blushing steppe flowers. Friar Carpini sums them up this way: "Their women are chaste, and one never hears scandals about them, though they tell coarse and vulgar jokes. . . . Sometimes they become quite drunk, yet while drunk they never fight with words or blows."[47]

The Mongol "First Family"

Though Genghis Khan ruled an empire of 100 million people, his imperial court was also a family affair. As head of a clan, he was bound by honor to fulfill the obligations of a chief. That meant settling quarrels, arranging

Hygiene

There's no way to disguise it: The Mongols were filthy. It was an article of their animistic religious belief that important spirits dwelt in rivers and streams and for that reason they refused to pollute water by washing in it. Due to the same prohibition, they also declined to wash their clothes, instead wearing them until they disintegrated. Nor did they wash their cooking utensils, beyond swirling a little meat broth in them.

The result was a stench that helped to foster the myth among the Muslims of the Mideast and the Christians of Europe that Mongols were foul demons from the bowels of hell.

Conquered foreign women reacted with revulsion to the vile odor of their Mongol tormentors. A haughty matriarch of the Naimans, one of the tribes subdued by Genghis Khan during his campaign to unify the peoples of the steppe, dismissed them as those "whose scent is bad" and went on to declare that the most delicate princess among them might be worthy to milk her goats, the low animal on the Mongol livestock totem pole, if she washed her hands thoroughly. Later, according to *The Secret History*, as Genghis was about to force himself on her, he taunted her with the words, "Did you not say that the Mongols had a bad scent? Why then have you come to me?"

marriages, dispensing favors, and keeping his five hundred wives happy.

When dealing with matters of state, he was often arbitrary and dictatorial, but when family concerns were the issue, he behaved in a more fatherly way. The Persian historian Juvaini gives a glimpse of his style in this description of how he used a homespun metaphor to teach his fractious sons the importance of sticking together:

He drew an arrow from his quiver and gave it to his sons. Clearly it required great strength to break it. He made the number two [added a second arrow] and continued until there were fourteen, and even athletes were unable to break them. "So it is," he said, "with respect to my sons also. So long as they tread the path of regard for one another they shall be secure from the evils of events and shall be free to enjoy the fruits of their kingdom."[48]

Genghis wasn't always so gentle when he turned his attention to family affairs. To be chosen as a son-in-law by the emperor was considered a great honor, but it turned out to be a curse rather than a blessing for one young tribal prince who thought the daughter Genghis had offered him as a bride was somewhat lacking in looks. The haughty young man's ill-considered response ignited the wrath of the Khan. "Your daughter," he said, "looks like a frog and a tortoise. How can I accept her?"[49] Before he had a chance to elaborate, his head was rolling in the dust.

The equality that steppe life afforded women in the nomadic family extended to the imperial court. As Genghis sat on his throne, deciding the fate of thousands with a mere gesture of his hand, his favorite wives sat to his left, carefully positioned in descending order of seniority from Borte down to the most

recent prized acquisition. They were vocal advisers, whose words the Khan listened to with the same attention as those of his darkhans and military commanders.

The Secret History contains snide references to the influence Genghis' wives had over him, stopping just short of calling him henpecked. Even his mother, Hoelun, got into the act—in a very dramatic way. During one debate, when she felt she was being ignored, she bared her breasts to get his attention. The ploy worked as well in the Khan's ger as it would in a twenty-first-century boardroom.

A Durable, Long Lasting Base

The Mongol family was a strong social institution. It withstood centuries of tribal warfare on the steppe and adapted without difficulty to the reforms that Genghis carried out when he transformed the Mongol tribe into the hub of an empire that stretched from one end of Asia to the other.

Neither the frequent famines that swept the steppe nor the uncertain fortunes of war were able to shake its foundations. Its strength lay in its self-sufficiency. A smaller, more nuclear family, with fewer resources to draw on, would have been crushed by these tides of history. The Mongol family, because it embraced several wives along with their children and relatives, had a broader and more durable base. The relatively high degree of equality between the sexes also contributed to the family's security. If the father died an untimely death in battle, his wives, with the support of their children and relatives, could carry on without him. The strength and unity of the family transcended even death. The Mongols believed that the spirits of their ancestors were always near at hand to guide and protect them. In fact, ancestor worship was one of the cornerstones of their rich spiritual life.

Shamans and the Spirit World

The Mongol spiritual universe was a crowded place, populated by gods and spirits beyond number. Trees, rocks, mountains, rivers, and animals were all full of spirits. The spirits of ancestors hovered around the families they left behind. Whenever a Mongol fell ill, one or more of these spirits had to be appeased. When an undertaking of any importance was on the drawing board, gods and spirits had to be consulted and their support enlisted.

Literally, no aspect of daily life was exempt from at least a passing acknowledgment that the gods and spirits were watching. When a new flask of kumiss was opened, the first drink was offered to the gods; before the first morsel of food was eaten, a portion was set aside for the gods. At a special place behind the fire pit, each ger had a shrine to the family's ancestor gods. Felt idols, made by women and women only, presided over the events of the day, and no day started without a prayer and a sacrifice to keep the ancestor spirits happy.

Some spirits were more powerful than others; some were accessible to every man and woman, but others—stronger, more distant, maybe more sinister—could be safely approached only by someone trained in the strange and mysterious art of spiritual diplomacy. These were the shamans. The Mongol religion had no priestly class, no churches, no hierarchy. The entire world was a temple and the gods and spirits weren't confined to a remote realm. They lived among men and intruded into the most mundane activities.

The shamans were specialists in dealing with this complex array of gods and ghosts and, as such, attained positions of immense power among the tribes and clans. They not only officiated at major rites of passage, such as weddings and burials, but were fully integrated into the fabric of every Mongol's life. Not even Genghis Khan himself made a move without their guidance and help.

One way Mongols acknowledged the gods was by offering them the first drink from a new flask of kumiss.

The need to propitiate so many gods and spirits gave rise to an intricate panoply of customs and rituals that every Mongol had to observe on pain of losing divine favor. These practices were taken so seriously that transgressions were frequently punished by death. The Mongols regarded showing respect to the spirit world to be a matter of collective responsibility. If an individual offended an animal spirit, the whole clan might have to pay the price in the form of an unsuccessful hunt or a drought that would decimate the herds. It was an article of their religious faith that if a tribal member transgressed, others could well starve to death. The damage caused by these transgressions could, in some instances, be repaired by an adept shaman, but the surest form of atonement was to swiftly punish the transgressor in the hope that this act of spiritual "law enforcement" would spare the whole tribe from the wrath of the outraged spirit or god.

Father Sky

Koeke Moengki Tengri, Eternal Blue Heaven, was the principal god of the Mongols. Although he was believed to have had divine sons, he was not worshiped as an anthropomorphic god-man with an individual personality. Rather, Tengri was more an overarching universal spiritual presence that infused all things and through which all things derived their being.

Although impersonal, Tengri governed everything that happened in the world and preserved the balance of the universe. And although he had no personal will, he could decidedly and decisively influence the outcome of events, so sacrifices were routinely made to ensure his favor. Genghis Khan prefaced all his official pronouncements, called biliks, with the words "by the will of Eternal Blue Heaven"[50] in order to entice Tengri's support.

Whenever Genghis Khan embarked on his military campaigns he first consulted the gods.

The god was regarded as the protector of all the peoples of the steppe and rulers felt their authority derived from him. From the Mongols' point of view, Tengri governed the entire earth, and when Genghis embarked on his conquests he believed that he had a divine mission to embrace the entire population of the world into his god's universal tribe. Over time, Genghis came to be referred to as the "son of Tengri" a concept the Mongols derived from the Chinese, who called their emperor the "son of heaven."

Tengri was not an elitist god; every Mongol, no matter how humble, could appeal to him directly. In fact, every Mongol carried the essence of Tengri within his body. According to Shaman South, a modern writer on shamanism, "The crown of the head, has a small piece of Tenger [another way in which Tengri's name is spelled] residing in it; it is the point of connection between the individual . . . and heaven above. This point receives energy from Tenger which flows down the center of a person's soul."[51]

Tengri expressed himself mainly through the weather. Lightning was a sure sign of his displeasure and rain was regarded as a divine blessing. Shamans spent much of their time enacting rituals to influence the meteorological manifestations of the god. Whenever lightning struck, for example, a shaman would be summoned to dance around the spot, chanting incantations to dampen Tengri's anger. Sunlight piercing through the clouds was taken as a sign that the god was pleased with his children.

Mother Earth and Other Mongol Gods

Tengri had a female counterpart named Gazan. Whereas he was worshiped as the sky god, she was revered as the earth goddess. Like him, she was not thought of anthropomorphically, but as the principle that nurtured and sustained the material conditions of life. In the Mongol pantheon of gods, she was held to be subordinate to Tengri.

Although Gazan had no physical form, like Tengri she had two children. In her case, they were daughters. She manifested herself in trees, a nurturing symbol in accord with her feminine persona, as opposed to Tengri's more masculine appearances in the violence of lightning. Writes Shaman South, "Like trees, all human beings draw strength from the Mother Earth below as well as receiving the energy of Father Heaven through the crown of the head."[52]

Gazan's special province was fertility, both of humans and of the herds, and she was worshiped with sacrifices. Tengri's sons were Uleg and Erleg, rulers of the upper and lower worlds, respectively. Gazan's daughters, Umai and Golomto, cared for hearth and home. The Mongols also prayed to the sun and moon—which they believed were the eyes of Tengri—as life-sustaining and regulating forces of the universe. The full moon was regarded as a particularly auspicious time to undertake important ventures.

The worship of the sun and moon gave the Mongols a circular concept of time, unlike the linear notion that has governed Western thinking. For them, history doesn't have a beginning, middle, and end, but flows continuously like the seasons of the year. Shaman South notes, "The cycles of the sun and moon demonstrate the circularity of time and all other natural processes. . . . Time circles around infinitely, so that each point in time is in contact with every other."[53]

Three Worlds and Three Souls

The Mongols divided the cosmos into three regions: the upper, lower, and middle worlds. Living beings inhabited the middle realm, the everyday world we all live in. The lower world was remarkably like the middle one. It had rivers and trees, good and bad weather, all the features of ordinary life. It was located beneath the surface of the earth and was linked to the middle world physically by rivers, streams, eddies, and caves. It was also the realm of the spirits of those who had died, waiting to be reincarnated in new physical forms.

The Case of the Meddling Shaman

A shaman named Teb-Tengri (Most Heavenly) wormed his way into young Genghis Khan's heart by wandering naked through the wilderness loudly proclaiming that the Sky God himself had appeared to him in a vision prophesying future greatness for the up-and-coming warlord. As susceptible as any Mongol to the oracular pronouncements of shamans, Genghis appointed Teb-Tengri to be his personal spiritual guide.

But, like many other shamans, Teb-Tengri had political aspirations of his own. Even the Khan's throne itself was not beyond his power-hungry dreams. He spread lies to sow discontent between Genghis and his family, whispering that divine favor had shifted to Genghis's half-brother Kasar. A feud erupted and Genghis made up his mind to execute Kasar. Only their mother's last-minute intervention prevented bloodshed.

It took a lot of convincing to shake Genghis's faith in his shaman, but when he realized his own interests were at stake he was quick to act. Three of his henchmen ambushed the conniving shaman and broke his back. Practicality easily won out over religious scruples.

In the Mongol version of reincarnation, the souls of men and women returned in the bodies of men and women, those of bears as bears, and so on. However, some souls of still-living beings could become separated from their bodies by sickness or madness and end up in the underworld before their time. One of the shaman's most important roles was to travel to the lower world and negotiate with its ruler Erleg for the return of these trapped spirits.

The upper world lay beyond the sky. It, too, was like the middle world, except that it was brighter. In one myth, it has seven suns. "Descriptions of the upper world say that it resembles the earth, but nature in that world is still unspoiled and its inhabitants still live in the traditional ways of the ancestors,"[54] writes Shaman South. Only the souls of very powerful people went to the upper world, and once there they were no longer subject to reincarnation.

All three worlds were joined by a central axis, symbolized by the imaginary line that runs from the fire in the center of the ger through the opening in the top of the tent all the way to the sky. The smoke that rose from the fire was believed to be a sacred representation of this mythical pole that held the three-tiered cosmos together. Trees also served this symbolic function and both were routes along which the shaman mystically moved from the middle world to the others.

Parallel to the three-part structure of the cosmos, the Mongols believed that living human beings had three souls. The ami soul, or breathing soul, animated the body and sustained the physical aspects of life. It was also the seat of mental powers—reason, language, even psychic abilities—and it was reincarnated. Animals, as well as humans, had ami souls. This belief in the reincarnation of animal souls gave rise to the Mongol custom of killing prey and slaughtering livestock with the greatest reverence. If the animal spirit was offended, they reasoned, it would not return in a new body and the result would be poor hunts, dwindling herds and, ultimately, starvation. Battle-hardened Mongol warriors were known to weep after killing a deer—an

Inside their ger, Mongols gathered around the shrine and prayed to their ancestors' spirits.

outpouring of emotion that did not extend to their human victims.

The suld soul, where the individual personality resided, left the body at death and was not reincarnated. These were the souls that hovered around the ger as helper spirits, the ones that were prayed to during the rituals of ancestor worship and whose idols were the object of reverence among the Mongols. The suns soul also contributed to an individual's personality and it is also where the memory of past lives resided. It was the suns soul that traveled to the underworld after a person died to await reincarnation.

Spirits, Spirits, and More Spirits

Ancestor spirits were of particular importance to the Mongols. Every ger had a shrine in a place of honor to the north side of the fire, usually a bench or table, which housed idols of the family's honored dead. Every morning the family prayed to these ancestor idols to enlist their support in the day's undertakings. Before mealtime, their lips were daubed with the fat of the meat in a grace offering. The first sip of milk or of kumiss was always ritually poured in front of the shrine, one of the few occasions when the Mongols tolerated waste of any kind. When an animal was slaughtered for food, its heart was cut out and left overnight before the ancestor idols, then eaten. Through rituals like these, the Mongols maintained an extended spiritual family that was just as important to them as their flesh-and-blood relatives.

When the Mongols looked at nature, they saw spirits with willful, conscious intent to which they appealed through prayer and sacrifice in a bid to harness the power of nature to meet their needs. No mere mortal, no matter how mighty, dared to ignore the unpredictable powers of nature spirits. Genghis Khan, and no mortal Mongol was more powerful than he, was no exception.

This account from *The Secret History* describes him praying to the spirit of a mountain. After confessing that his life was no more significant than that of a grasshopper in the face of the mountain's mystic majesty, he declared: "I was caused to be sore afraid. Every morning I shall sacrifice unto Mount Barquan. Every day I shall pray unto it." Then, the account continues, the Great Khan "hanged his girdle on his neck, hanged his hat in his hand [his belt and hat were symbols of his earthly authority], struck his hand into his breast, and, kneeling nine times toward the sun, offered a sprinkling of mare's milk and a prayer."[55] Similar rituals were repeated daily by all Mongols.

The Mongol attitude toward the spirit world was one of profound respect. Mongols drew no sharp distinction between the natural world and the realm of the spirits. Spirit worship was simply one of the practicalities of life. Just as a Mongol would not be foolish enough to go into battle without first sharpening his sword, so too he would not be reckless enough to risk his life without first taking steps to ensure that the relevant spirits were on his side, or at least neutralized. As reverent as they were to their gods and the spirits, their innate practicality infused their religious life. The gods and spirits could be forces for good or evil, they could work for or against any individual in any situation. The path of prudence dictated that they be kept happy.

The Shaman as Spirit Guide and Healer

Shamans were necessary to keep the gods and spirits happy. Through a process of divine selection and intensive training, the shamans acquired occult powers that equipped them to travel in the spiritual realm and communicate with its inhabitants. Untrained people became aware of the presence of a spirit by indirect means, the crackling of a fire or the whistling of the wind, for example—but shamans could actually see the ghostly presences with their eyes and could enter into direct, verbal negotiations with them.

Because of their special abilities, shamans were held in high esteem and exerted great power among the Mongols, even in the court of the Khan. They were the medicine men called in to cure the sick. Illness was held to have two basic causes: either an offended spirit was seeking revenge or the ailing person's suld or suns soul had become temporarily separated

Two Views of Death

For the Mongols, there was death and then there was death. Death in battle, they took in stride. They knew what caused it and accepted that they were vulnerable to it every time they faced an enemy. But death due to sickness filled them with dread. It was the work of spirits, whose evil could contaminate others. Other inhabitants of the ger of a dying person had to be purified by walking between two fires. Shamans were called to make sure the souls of the dead were appeased and would help rather than harm the living.

The afterlife was pictured in terms that were very this-worldly. The dead were buried with their possessions and offerings of food. Sometimes they were even buried in their gers. A pregnant mare was sacrificed to provide the departed with a spiritual herd. In the case of a powerful chief, young women were sacrificed so that his spirit would not be lonely.

from his body due to failure to observe the rituals and sacrifices that kept the forces of nature in balance. In the first case, the shaman performed rituals and incantations to appease the disgruntled spirit. In the latter, occult powers enabled him or her to travel to the underworld and negotiate the return of the wayward soul. In both cases, the shaman communicated with the relevant gods and spirits while in a trance, induced by dancing, chanting, and—in some cases, but certainly not all—by consuming hallucinogenic herbs.

If the shaman's destination was the lower world, he or she traveled a perilous mystical route through rivers and streams. If the destination was the upper world, shamans ascended on flying white horses or climbed a tree symbolizing the World Tree that leads beyond heaven. On arrival, they had to use all their wiles and powers of persuasion to get the relevant god or spirit to the negotiating table. They promised sacrifices and prayers on behalf of those they were representing, cajoled, flattered, even resorted to trickery to get the spirit counterpart to come to terms.

Once the negotiations were complete, the shamans returned to the middle world (came out of their trances) and, after checking on the condition of the patient, either accepted praise and gifts for his success or blamed the magnitude of the offense or the stubbornness of the god or spirit for his failure.

The Shaman as Seer

Shamans also foretold the future by reading omens. They held the shoulder bone of a sheep and asked a question, then threw the bone into a fire, where it burned until it charred and cracked. If it cracked in a uniform manner along the length of the bone, the answer to the question was deemed to be positive. But if it cracked in a random way or across the bone, the signs were deemed adverse.

The prophetic function was one of the shaman's most important, particularly when battles were being planned. An awkwardly

Held in high esteem, the shaman, a spiritual adviser, exerted a great deal of influence among the Mongols.

cracked bone could be enough to cancel a whole campaign, but if the matter at hand was very important, it frequently happened that many bones were burned until a majority of the evidence gave the desired answer. Practicality, as always, weighed at least as heavily as the cosmic will.

The Mongols were so avid to know the future that soothsaying was not confined to the shamans. Genghis Khan himself used to practice it, comparing his results with those of the shamans. On the eve of any major undertaking, it was his habit to go into a trance and have a scribe record whatever he said in this altered state of consciousness. When he returned to his normal frame of mind, his pronouncements were read back to him and formed the basis of his decisions. Once, before an important battle in China, he shut himself up in his tent for four days to commune with the spirits while his devoted followers were required to fast and chant the name of Tengri outside.

In the words of the Indian chronicler Juzjani, Genghis was

an adept at magic and deception, and some of the devils were his friends. Every now and again he used to fall into a trance, and in that state of insensibility all sorts of things used to proceed from his tongue. . . . Whenever this inspiration came over him, every circumstance—victories, undertakings, the appearance of enemies, the defeat and reduction of countries—anything which he might desire, would all be uttered by his tongue. A person used to take the whole down in writing and enclose it in a bag and place a seal upon it, and when Genghis Khan came to his senses again, they used to read his utterances over to him one by one: and according to these he would act,

Genghis Khan, pictured here, attempts to see into the future through the practice of soothsaying.

and more or less, indeed, the whole use to come true.[56]

The shamans were so pivotal to Mongol life they often exerted a great deal of political control, either directly by becoming tribal leaders or clan chiefs themselves or indirectly by influencing others. No leader could afford to flaunt the prophecies and pronouncements of a respected shaman on pain of losing the confidence of his people. Shamans exploited the authority they wielded and the unscrupulous ones used it to increase their personal wealth.

The Shaman as Showman

Shamans also played a dramatic role in the cultural lives of the Mongols. In fact, they were the society's principal entertainers. Shamans didn't mumble their prayers and incantations. They sang them with gusto, often with musical accompaniment. When they worked themselves into trances, they didn't do it sitting silently with their faces to the wall of a ger. They danced frenetically until they worked themselves into states of ecstasy. And they adorned themselves extravagantly in animal masks and colorful feathers.

The shamans never had trouble holding the attention of their audiences. Since the dramas they acted out with such exuberance dealt with the fate and fortune of their spectators, their every word and gesture was greeted with awe. Success, after all, wasn't measured in mere applause, but in life and death, in victory and defeat, in plenty or starvation—in the very balance of the cosmos itself. The shaman's costars also guaranteed a captivated audience. They weren't simply other actors, but gods and goddesses and powerful spirits, who could be seen by the shaman only, but sensed by everyone through his cathartic performance.

The showmanship of shamanism wasn't merely an entertaining side effect. A shaman's stature depended on the trust he or she inspired. Therefore, through the performance of rituals, shamans had to convince their audiences of the realism of their journeys into the spirit realm. When they wrestled with evil spirits, for example, they had to convey the epic nature of the struggle through physical gestures and this required intense powers of concentration and athletic bodily control.

The Windhorse

The purpose of life for the Mongols was to live in harmony with nature and the cosmos. Those who achieved this balance through ethical living and the observance of religious rituals were rewarded with an increase in their personal power. Called himori, or windhorse, this power was thought to be a physical substance that resided in the chest. Right living caused windhorse to accumulate; wrong living dissipated one's supply. Those whose windhorse was strong and plentiful had mental clarity and wisdom and could discern the truth through clouds of deception. They could also accomplish great deeds effortlessly and attract others through the force of their personalities. Needless to say, Genghis Khan was believed to have had an abundance of windhorse.

Shamans were praised—and paid—for their leaping ability, the suppleness of their contortions, and their capacity to feign death by lying perfectly motionless. Each of the shamans' roles—prophecy, healing, sacrificing, spirit travel—entailed specific rituals they were required to perform. Over time, these became more and more elaborate, evolving into highly complex performances. As one shaman attempted to outdo others, he or she added variations on the central theme, much in the same way an actor injects his own personality into the characters he plays.

In their role as performers, the shamans required almost superhuman stamina. Some of the rituals lasted for three days and required them to climb trees, reenact cosmic chases, and engage in protracted wrestling matches with demons. If the ritual involved sacrifice, they invited members of the audience to participate in killing and cooking the sacrificial animal. All of this was accompanied by nonstop chanting and drum beating, with the audience joining in. The shaman's props included his drum, his masks, usually of animals and birds, perhaps a horsehair fiddle and various feather headdresses, armbands, anklebands, and a mirror which, it was believed, enabled him or her to see spirits and the souls of the dead.

Many shamans, both male and female, were very old, but age didn't exempt them from the athletic performances their audiences demanded. The historian of religion Mircea Eliade describes the performance of an elderly shaman who won praise for leaping higher than his younger counterparts and who also "gashed himself with a knife, swallowed sticks, ate burning coals."[57] Thus the shaman had a repertoire of techniques and talents—singing, dancing, sword swallowing, fire eating—that would have made him or her a headliner on the vaudeville stages of the early twentieth century.

Religious Toleration

It is strange to attribute to the autocratic Mongols, who believed they were destined to rule the world, a characteristic as liberal as religious tolerance. Yet, they allowed the many religions they encountered during their conquests to coexist quite cheerfully with their native shamanism. Genghis granted religious freedom to all conquered peoples and even gave tax exemptions to their mosques, temples, and churches.

This tolerance presented no religious conflict for the Mongols. They were used

to worshiping multiple gods and one or two more didn't upset their belief system in any way. Politically, the policy gave Genghis a tremendous advantage by conscripting—a cynic might say bribing—local ecclesiastic officials to help the Mongols keep the native population under control. Although Genghis himself stayed true to his shamanistic roots, his successors freely embraced foreign faiths when it suited them.

Historian David Morgan describes this phenomenon as opportunistic. Regarding the

The Chuluut Gol River (pictured) is in the Mongolian People's Republic. Mongols were forbidden to bathe in rivers and streams because they were considered passageways to the spirit world.

casual attitude toward foreign religions that Genghis's sons and grandsons inherited, he writes:

> It was not long before they took the line of least resistance and adopted, in the various parts of their empire, a more developed religion learned from their conquered subjects. . . . Toleration there certainly was, but it was determined not so much by high-mindedness as by indifference, by a feeling that any religion might be right and that therefore it would be sensible to have every subject praying for the khan; and also by the fact that nomadic society in the steppes was accustomed to the practice of many religions.[58]

The Mongols' tolerance for other religions did have its limits, however. They banned practices that directly conflicted with their most deeply held beliefs. Genghis was outraged that Muslims didn't eat the remains of sacrificial animals, violating the Mongol taboo against waste. Their habit of taking ritual baths in rivers and streams also offended him because he believed it polluted the all-important passageways between this world and the one below, thus interfering with the ability of shamans to reclaim souls that had become separated from their bodies.

In general, the Mongols regarded the priests of other religions as just another type of shaman or sorcerer, whose powers could be harnessed for their own purposes. Thus, Genghis insisted that prayers be said for him in the mosques of Samarkand after he sacked that Islamic city—one has to wonder how heartfelt those prayers were—and turned to astrologers of all persuasions if he

thought they could give him a glimpse into the future. As a side note, he was particularly attentive to Islamic rites because he thought Muslims possessed prodigious sexual stamina, not a trivial matter for a man who had five hundred wives.

The self-serving motive behind the Mongol toleration of foreign religions is summed up by Harvard University historian Richard Foltz, writing about the point of view Genghis instilled in his grandson Mongke Khan:

> It is clear that in typical Mongol fashion, Mongke's policy was to support each religion equally in view of what powers they might provide. William [of Rubruck] mentions that on feast days, the clergy of each religion in turn would come before the khan to pray for him. . . . In William's somewhat cynical view, the khan "believes in none of them . . . and yet they all follow his court as flies do honey, and he makes them all gifts and all of them believe they are on intimate terms with him."[59]

Abiding Religious Faith

The Mongols' drew great strength from their religious beliefs. They were secure in their faith that they were all nurtured by Tengri, the Sky-God, and Gazan, the Earth Goddess. They were sure that their individual lives were watched over by protective ancestor spirits. They believed in the power of shamans to intercede with the gods and spirits on their behalf.

They also knew that if they observed the appropriate rituals and maintained an attitude of reverence, they would be in harmony with the universe and their endeavors would meet a happy fate. They believed that their leader, Genghis Khan, had been chosen by heaven to lead them into battle and that their obedience would be divinely rewarded. When they fought, they felt they were acting in harmony with the universe and that victory was guaranteed. This faith, as much as their hardiness and military skill, made them the unconquerable warriors they were.

Dancers, Wrestlers, and Storytellers

While the military accomplishments of the Mongols have been well chronicled, mostly by their defeated adversaries, their cultural life lays buried beneath the dry soil and scrub grass of the Central Asian steppe. Only cryptic evidence remains for historians to work with and even that has been warped by centuries of foreign intrusions.

Researchers have to grapple with three problems. First, the Mongols had no written language until Genghis adopted the Uiger script in the thirteenth century. Whereas their neighbors in China and the Muslim lands had been recording their cultural exploits in writing for countless generations, the Mongols passed theirs down by word of mouth. All written literature has its roots in an oral tradition—Homer's epics, for example, were recited by traveling storytellers for thousands of years before they were copied down. But that event happened relatively early in the history of the Greeks and gave subsequent scholars a body of ancient writings upon which to base their reconstructions of contemporary life.

With the Mongols, the situation is much different. Not until Russian and Chinese anthropologists began collecting folktales in the twentieth century did we have our first hints of what the oral literature of Genghis's time might have been like. Over the years, many foreign elements crept in and the work of sifting through the data is still in its early stages.

The second problem is that, as nomads whose lives depended on their mobility, the Mongols had little use for painting and sculpture. Carrying art treasures of that sort would have slowed them down and put their lives at

A Fable of Creation

Mongol storytellers gave this account of the creation of the middle world, the world in which we all live: Tengri had two sons: Ulgen, Lord of the Upper World, and Erleg, Lord of the Lower World. At that time, the earth was covered with water and there was no land. Ulgen asked the goldeneye duck to create land and the duck dragged up a small bit of mud from below and created a patch of land for Ulgen to sleep on. Erleg saw that his brother was asleep and tried to pull the land from under him. Instead, as he pulled, the land stretched out in all directions. Ulgen then created humans and animals from mud and laid them on the land to dry. He ordered the dog—then dogs could talk, but had no fur—to keep watch. Erleg tempted the dog away with a beautiful fur coat to shield him from the cold. When the dog had gone off admiring his shiny new coat, Erleg spat on the humans and animals and that is how disease and death came into the world. Ulgen saw what had happened and punished the dog by taking away his voice and ordaining that he would have to follow humans in order to get food to eat.

risk. Also, with the exception of Karakorum, they had no cities and hence no clearly defined places where archaeologists could search for remnants of their cultural achievements. The steppe is an overwhelming expanse of territory to comb for artifacts and those few historical diggers into the past who have struck pay dirt did so only with a great deal of luck on their side.

The nomadism of all the peoples of the steppe has clouded the archaeological record in a third way. As tribe after tribe swept across the vast plain, they all left traces, albeit meager ones, of their presence. Sorting out which group left which artifacts behind is a daunting task and the researcher always runs the risk of mistaking the remains of one people for those of another. The Mongols' fondness for plunder only adds to the confusion. Did they make a particular bowl themselves, for example, or did they loot it from a neighboring civilization?

Historian Rene Grousset recapitulates these problems and hints at another one: "Possessing neither stable settlements nor landed property, they remained strangers to statuary, bas-relief and painting. . . . Their lux-uries were confined to richness of dress and personal adornment, and to ornamentation of equipment, harness and so on."[60] In other words, the result of Mongol artistic endeavor was likely confined to objects made of textiles, wood, and leather—precisely the types of material that are most vulnerable to decay over time. So far, the picture looks pretty bleak, but it would be a serious mistake to dismiss the Mongols as barbarians who had no culture worthy of the name. The absence of cultural monuments doesn't necessarily imply the absence of culture altogether and we will see that the cultural life of the Mongols was surprisingly rich despite its lack of historical "footprints."

Singing and Dancing

Although the shaman was the principal entertainer among the Mongol people, singing and dancing were not confined to religious performances. They were an important part of secular activities as well and the Mongols were particularly fond of dancing to celebrate

Identifying this bowl as a Mongolian artifact from the Genghis Khan period is difficult because of the Mongol's habit of plundering other civilizations.

everything from weddings to battles. The style of dance was boisterous and exuberant, based on rhythmic hand, foot, and body contortions. *The Secret History* contains many accounts of dancing on festive occasions. After confirming the election of a new chief, one clan was said to have danced so long and so energetically they created a hole in the ground: "As for the rejoicing of the Mongyol, they were wont to rejoice, dancing and feasting. Having raised up Qutula as qa [chief], they danced about the Branching Tree [a prominent landmark] of Qorqonay Valley until there was a ditch up to their ribs; until there was dust up to their knees."[61]

Dancers, acrobats, and other performers were regularly featured in Genghis Khan's court.

In addition to this spontaneous dancing on festive occasions, semiprofessional dancers and acrobats entertained wealthy families in exchange for food or baubles. The practice started out informally among the tribes and clans of the steppe, where herdsmen with special talent or training performed for others, but when Genghis established himself as emperor traveling troupes of dancers, singers, and acrobats became a feature of court life. *The Secret History* alludes to these performers, but the best account of the Mongol taste in entertainment comes from Marco Polo, writing about a banquet hosted by Genghis's grandson Kublai Khan: "When they have fed and the tables are removed, a great troupe of jugglers and acrobats and other entertainers comes into the hall and performs remarkable feats of various kinds. And they all afford great amusement and entertainment in the Khan's presence, and the guests show their enjoyment by peals of laughter."[62]

But not even these showmen were exempt from the Mongol preoccupation with conquest. Polo tells how they were enlisted by Kublai to sack a city called Mien, which he wanted to add to his territories:

> The truth is that at his court there were a great number of jugglers and acrobats. The Khan told them that he wished them to go and conquer the province of Mien, and that he would give them a leader and supporting troops. The jugglers willingly accepted the charge and set out on their way. . . . What need of more words? Suffice it to say that these jugglers and their helpers conquered this province of Mien.[63]

Music also was a prominent feature of Mongol cultural life. Storytellers used it to add dramatic highlights to their recitations, but the Mongols also prized it for pure entertainment value. Singing contests were popular among many of the steppe peoples, including the Mongols. Rival minstrels competed with each other, exhibiting both their musical talent and the wit and grace of the lyrics of the songs they sang. Performers followed strict rules governing both musical structure and lyric versification. The losers often had to pay the winners, who were also rewarded by wealthy members of the audience.

Instruments in use included a type of fretless lute with two or three strings, the horsehair fiddle, wooden flutes, and drums. The songs themselves could be either quick-paced with a well-defined rhythmic structure or slow and protracted with a great deal of rhythmic latitude allowed to the performer. They were heterophonic, a technique common to the folk music of many cultures and which means simply that the main melodic line is repeated with numerous variations throughout the piece. The Mongol style of music spread widely over the steppe, carried from Manchuria in the east to the Volga River in the west by their restless armies. Singers, like Kublai's jugglers and acrobats, were frequently enlisted in imperial affairs. In 1289, the Mongol ruler of Persia sent a minstrel to negotiate with King Philip IV of France.

Art and Architecture

Though it is difficult to distinguish artifacts made by the Mongols from those they plundered, the archaeological record does give some indication of what they valued in aesthetic terms. Gold ornaments and brocade fabrics were highly prized, as were intricate designs with animal and floral motifs. One of the most striking finds is a stunning gold saddle facing dating to Genghis's time. Art historian Adam Kessler says the facing and other saddle ornaments "were retrieved from the tomb of a Mongol noblewoman who was 17 to 19 years old at the time of her death. They were made of hammered gold leaf and designed to fit over a wooden saddle. The central motif of the front arch ornament is a reclining deer."[64]

Other excavated graves have yielded gold cups and ladles with similar patterns and a number of intricately woven gold brocade garments, either purloined from vanquished enemies or fabricated by enslaved craftsmen from foreign lands. We know that items such as these were prized by the Mongols, who hoarded them both for their value as status symbols and for their real economic worth in barter transactions. Genghis liked to reward faithful followers with gold artifacts seized during his military campaigns and used them to make a boastful show of his generosity.

As for indigenous Mongol artifacts, only a smattering of belt buckles, knives, and saddle ornaments have been unearthed. Some of these are in silver, but most are made of iron or carved wood. Some samples of decorative needlework on saddles, harnesses, and boots have been found, as have outlandish hats worn by noblewomen as symbols of status, but the archeological evidence of native Mongol craftsmanship is very thin. Many discoveries, in fact, bear the unmistakable stamp of Chinese or Islamic artisans.

One other example of Mongol art deserves mention: the imperial seals, a number of which have been found by archaeologists. These were made of bronze and inscribed with a decorative script indicating that the people bearing them were on official business and should in no way be hindered from carrying out their duties. Most likely, because they carry written instructions, they were made by the foreign secretaries who documented the administration of the empire.

Huge granite tortoises sit outside the walled city of Karakorum, one of the few remainders of the 13th century Mongol Empire.

Architecturally, the Mongols were predictably primitive compared to the settled civilizations that surrounded them. Their only city, Karakorum, was excavated by Russian archaeologists in 1948 and 1949. In the thirteenth century, cities like Paris, London, and Rome were thriving metropolises, but Karakorum was nothing more than a humble, mud-walled village. The Khan's palace sat on a platform of raised earth and measured a modest 820 feet by 740 feet. The walls were made of clay, sand, and pebbles and stood 16 feet high, surrounding a central courtyard that contained the imperial residence and several other buildings. Archaeologists found tiles, glazed ornaments, pottery, coins, and some needlework but little else to reflect the scope of the Mongol empire at the height of its glory. Artistically, the only things of interest to survive are a pair of huge granite tortoises that flanked the east gate. Most of the rest of the original materials were used to build a

Buddhist lamasary near the site in the sixteenth century.

Folktales and Fables

Storytelling is the oldest Mongolian art form. As a nonliterate people, only their tales and legends, handed down from one generation to the next, preserved their history, traditions, and identity. Storytelling took many forms, from simple instructional yarns told by grandmothers to grandchildren, to elaborate verse epics sung by shamans and traveling troubadours.

Pureviin Khorloo, a native Mongolian scholar who has spent his life collecting folktales, explains how storytelling occupies a unique place in the history of his people:

Music, poetry, epics, folktales and regular speech do not have the same clear dividing lines in Mongolia that they perhaps have elsewhere. The verbal arts were among our earliest arts and have been paramount in this country of nomads. In the Mongolian culture, great stress has been placed upon personal skills, in particular intellectual skills, oratorical skills, and all kinds of verbal and vocal arts. As a nomadic people moving from place to place on the steppe, it was necessary that baggage be as light as possible. One's main assets included a finely honed ability to express oneself. . . . As a result, the verbal arts in Mongolia have included a great appreciation for rhythm, alliteration, all the aurally pleasing devices that can be used to communicate the range of human emotions. In Mongolia, songs, poetry and folktales were not related to writing until much later in their development than in agrarian societies. Folktales, proverbs and songs had a tremendous importance in daily life.[65]

Although storytellers were generally the elders of the clan or tribe, anyone who knew a good tale and had the ability to tell it well was allowed to do so. The heroic epics, the longest tales in the storyteller's repertoire, were usually sung or chanted to the accompaniment of a horsehair fiddle. Depending on the customs of individual tribes, storytellers were sometimes men, sometimes women. They came from no special class and formed no unique social subgroup, but they were surrounded by an aura of mystery and grandeur due to the storehouse of tribal lore they possessed.

According to Khorloo, the stories fell into more or less distinct categories:

Why the Mongols Tell Stories

This folktale is among those collected by Hilary Roe Metternich in her book *Mongolian Folktales*:

A fearful plague descended on the Mongol people. Many died and the others fled for their lives. A 10-year-old boy named Tarvaa struggled with Death for days. When he finally lost consciousness, his spirit thought he had died, left his body and journeyed to the Lower World. Surprised to see such a young spirit, Erleg demanded: "Why did you leave your body while it was still alive? Why are you here in my Kingdom?" With a trembling voice, Tarvaa responded: "All my family and all my friends who remained in that World stood over my body and said I was dead. Then they ran away. I did not wait for the terrible last moment, but simply left on my journey to you." Touched, the Lord of the Lower World told Tarvaa's spirit that his time had not yet come and sent him back to his body. But before leaving, the spirit was allowed to choose one gift from all the riches of the Lower World to bring with him. After looking among Wealth, Honor and many other treasures, he chose Tales and Legends. With Erleg's blessing the spirit returned to the World, but by the time he arrived a crow had already plucked the eyes from Tarvaa's lifeless body. The spirit dared not disobey Erleg and entered the body despite its sad condition. Though blind, Tarvaa lived for many years and traveled to the far corners of the Mongol land, telling his Tales and Legends wherever he went.

Mongolian folktales have been classified by those who have studied them into the following five general groups: those about animals, those about magic and especially the magical horse, those about domestic affairs, satirical tales, and, lastly, tales about relations between man and nature or about the origins of nature. This last category is believed to be the most ancient.[66]

The most frequently recurring theme is that of the horse, reflecting its crucial importance in all aspects of Mongol life. It is often portrayed as bringing good fortune, health, or supernatural powers. Other animals usually represent human attributes. The deer, for example, is a symbol of dishonesty and unreliability while the badger represents cunning.

Snakes are universally negative in their connotations, but lions, elephants, and dragons portray strength and goodness. The domestic tales, as their name implies, deal with the relationships between people and are often humorous; the satires are aimed at those who usurp authority and intrude unfairly into the lives of others; and the nature stories reflect the importance of the balance between man and his natural environment in the religious worldview of the Mongols.

Sports and Tests of Skill

As a people whose lives were a constant battle against nature, the Mongols placed a high value on physical strength and stamina and this is reflected in their choice of sports and

Falconry was a favorite sport among Mongols.

pastimes. Riding, archery contests, and hunting competitions were part of every child's education. All of these sports carried over into adulthood, when men would vie to see who possessed the skills of everyday life to the highest degree. Falconry was a favored sport among the wealthy and experienced hunting birds were considered to be among the most fitting gifts to exchange. Genghis always looked favorably upon supplicants who included a falcon among the gifts required to get him to focus his attention on their concerns.

But if the Mongols could be said to have had a favorite sport, that sport was wrestling. *The Secret History* reports that each clan had its champion and they were pitted against each other in friendly competitions when the various wandering groups gathered at the winter grazing grounds. The matches were no-holds-barred events, lasting until one of the combatants was clearly beaten or so badly injured he could not continue.

Wrestling had another function, however, one far less innocent. It was a mechanism used to settle disputes without resorting to full-scale bloodshed. Such "grudge matches" often ended in severe injury or even death when one of the wrestlers had his back broken.

When wrestling and drinking, another favorite Mongol hobby, were mingled, the results were often disastrous. *The Secret History* tells the story of a feast that turned into a donnybrook when a steward committed a breach of etiquette by pouring kumiss for a minor wife of one of the guests before serving the senior wife. A dispute erupted that was to be settled by a wrestling match between Genghis Khan's brother Beleugetai and the champion of the Juchid tribe, a formidable grappler called Bori. Beleugetai lost the match, but when he claimed he had been un-

Women and Wrestling

The following account by Marco Polo reveals the importance of wrestling and the far-from-acquiescent position of women in Mongol life. A Tatar princess named Kaidu had been given permission by her father to choose her own husband:

She made it known in many parts of the world that any youth of gentle birth might come and try his strength with her and if he could vanquish her she would take him as her husband. . . . This was the bargain: if the youth could so far vanquish her as to force her to the ground, he should have her to wife; if she vanquished him, he must forfeit a hundred horses to her. In this way she gained more than 10,000 horses. For never a squire or a gallant could she find who was a match for her. And no wonder; for she was so well-formed in every limb, so big-built, and so strapping, that she was little short of a giantess.

fairly tripped the banquet exploded into a melee in which even the normally reserved Genghis took part. Sober heads prevailed and the incident ended without bloodshed.

But Genghis had a long memory for insults and arranged another match. This time Beleugetai got the upper hand and at a key point looked towards his brother who gave him a sign to avenge the previous slight. "Beleugtai looked back," writes the author of *The Secret History*, "and, with his seeing Genghis Khan, the Khan bit his lower lip. Beleugetai, getting understanding, sat on top of him [Bori] . . . and, putting his knee on his backbone, [broke] it and dispatched him."[67] The Mongols played rough.

A Practical People

Mongol culture reflected the harshness of their nomadic life and their love of battle. Like the people themselves, it was rude, crude, and functional. Just as they abhorred wasting food and water, the Mongols were economical of their time. If an artifact or pastime had no practical value, they had little use for it.

Thus the few archeological treasures found pertain mostly to riding, hunting, battle, and the administration of the Khan's court. Communal singing and dancing promoted cohesiveness and cooperation. Storytelling instilled in children a sense of what it meant to be a Mongol and what would be expected of them when they grew older.

Even when they were spectators, the Mongols loved to watch performances that celebrated physical prowess. They valued agile, energetic dancers and strong, fearless wrestlers. The Mongols played as they lived—without restraint.

The End of Mongol Dominance

Genghis Khan died in 1227 after falling from his horse during a military campaign in China. He was sixty years old. Custom dictated that he be buried in the Mongolian homeland so that his spirit could dwell among his people and guide them. As the cortége bearing his body wended its way northward, all who witnessed its passing were put to death so their souls could keep his company in the afterlife. As with all great Mongol chiefs, Genghis was buried in a secret place, probably on the top of a hill so that he would be close to heaven. His grave has never been found, nor has the burial site of the sixty horses and sixty virgin girls who were sacrificed to provide him with a herd and a harem for all eternity.

Genghis had four sons, who inherited the empire he had created and also his drive to expand its borders. In accordance with the Mongol laws of inheritance, because his oldest son, Jochi, died shortly before his father, Jochi's son Batu was granted the lands farthest from the Mongol heartland—in this case the western part of the Eurasian steppe up to the border of Russia. Batu, aided by Genghis's most trusted generals, invaded Europe and, most historians agree, could have swept all the way to the Atlantic Ocean had western Europe provided enough pasture to sustain the horses of his vast Golden Horde, as the Mongols under his command were known. He withdrew to the steppe east of Russia and his successors continued to exact tribute from the Rus-

sians until Czar Ivan III drove them away in 1480.

The Great Khan's second son, Chagatai, and his family, ruled the territory north of Tibet, India, and Paskistan, extending as far west as the Aral Sea. Their domination began to wane in the fourteenth century. Genghis' third son, Ogodei, who succeeded him as Great Khan governed the lands comprising

Genghis Khan's four sons (pictured) inherited his empire.

Mongolia, Manchuria, Korea, and northern China. Ogodei's nephews, Mangu and Kublai, pushed the frontier of the empire southward and in 1279 Kublai established himself as head of the Yuan dynasty in China. Less than one hundred years later, the Mongols were ousted by the Ming dynasty and driven back onto the steppe.

Genghis's youngest son, Tolui, died six years after his father in 1233, but he had established a foothold for the Mongols in Islamic world, particularly in the area of modern-day Iran and Iraq. In 1258, his son Hulegu captured the city of Baghdad. The Mongols who ruled this territory quickly adopted the religion and culture of the people they had conquered. The Il-Khanate, as this part of the empire was called, dissolved into a number of smaller Iranian-ruled territories towards the end of the fourteenth century.

The Mongols' religious tolerance and fascination with luxuries made them susceptible to the influences of the civilizations they conquered. They tended to abandon the nomadic heritage that had made them so strong. They settled into the way of life of those around

Modern Mongolia

them, sacrificing the mobility that gave them their military superiority. Once that happened, it was easy for the conquered peoples to regroup and expel them.

Within little more than one hundred years of Genghis Khan's death, the Mongols, divorced from their nomadic and tribal roots, were driven back onto the steppe from which they had come. They never again played a major role in world history.

Notes

Chapter 1: Nomads of the Steppe

1. Paul Ratchnevsky, *Genghis Khan: His Life and Legacy*. Trans. Thomas Nivison Haining. Cambridge, MA: Blackwell, 1991, p. 19.
2. David Christian, *A History of Russia, Central Asia, and Mongolia*, vol. 1, *Inner Eurasia from Prehistory to the Mongol Empire*. Cambridge, MA: Blackwell, 1998, p. 15.
3. Rene Grousset, *The Empire of the Steppes: A History of Central Asia*. Trans. Naomi Walford. New Brunswick, NJ: Rutgers University Press, 1970, p. xxvi.
4. Christian, *A History of Russia, Central Asia, and Mongolia*, p. 413.
5. Grousset, *The Empire of the Steppes*, p. vii.
6. Friar Giovanni DiPlano Carpini, *The Story of the Mongols Whom We Call the Tartars*. Trans. Erik Hildinger. Boston: Branden, 1996, p. 41.
7. Quoted in Christian, *A History of Russia, Central Asia, and Mongolia*, p. 228.
8. Quoted in Ratchnevsky, *Genghis Khan*, p. 154.
9. Quoted in Christian, *A History of Russia, Central Asia, and Mongolia*, p. 398.

Chapter 2: Families, Clans, and Tribes

10. Quoted in Ratchnevsky, *Genghis Khan*, p. 12.
11. Christian, *A History of Russia, Central Asia, and Mongolia*, p. 88.
12. David Morgan, *The Mongols*. Malden, MA: Blackwell, 1986, p. 39.
13. Morgan, *The Mongols*, p. 39.

14. Morgan, *The Mongols*, p. 59.
15. Morgan, *The Mongols*, p. 37.
16. Morgan, *The Mongols*, p. 38.
17. Anonymous, *The Secret History of the Mongols*. Trans. Francis Woodman Cleaves. Cambridge, MA: Harvard University Press, 1982, p. 3.
18. Christian, *A History of Russia, Central Asia and Mongolia*, p. 422.
19. Ratchnevsky, *Genghis Khan*, p. 13.
20. Ratchnevsky, *Genghis Khan*, pp. 19–20.
21. Anonymous, *The Secret History of the Mongols*, p. 140.

Chapter 3: Genghis Khan's Reforms

22. Christian, *A History of Russia, Central Asia, and Mongolia*, pp. 398-99.
23. Grousset, *The Empire of the Steppes*, p. 221.
24. Charles J. Halperin, *Russia and the Golden Horde: The Mongol Impact on Medieval Russian History*. Bloomington: Indiana University Press, 1985, p. 25.
25. Quoted in Grousset, *The Empire of the Steppes*, p. 249.
26. Quoted in Grousset, *The Empire of the Steppes*, p. 231.
27. Quoted in Ratchnevsky, *Genghis Khan*, p. 150.
28. Quoted in Ratchnevsky, *Genghis Khan*, p. 159.
29. Ratchnevsky, *Genghis Khan*, p. xvi.

Chapter 4: The Mongol War Machine

30. S. R. Turnbull, *The Mongols*. Oxford: Osprey, 1980, p. 3.
31. Turnbull, *The Mongols*, p. 17.
32. Carpini, *The Story of the Mongols*, p. 89.
33. Marco Polo, *The Travels*. Trans. Ronald Latham. London: Penguin, 1958, p. 99.

34. Carpini, *The Story of the Mongols*, p. 52.
35. Polo, *The Travels*, p. 99.
36. Carpini, *The Story of the Mongols*, pp. 71–72.
37. Anonymous, *The Secret History of the Mongols*, p. 55.
38. Polo, *The Travels*, p. 101.
39. Morgan, *The Mongols*, p. 122.
40. Christian, *A History of Russia, Central Asia, and Mongolia*, p. 144.

Chapter 5: Husbands, Wives, and Children

41. Carpini, *The Story of the Mongols,* p. 54.
42. Christian, *A History of Russia, Central Asia, and Mongolia*, p. 87.
43. Carpini, *The Story of the Mongols,* p. 54.
44. Anonymous, *The Secret History of the Mongols*, p. 45.
45. Polo, *The Travels*, p. 98.
46. Polo, *The Travels*, p. 98.
47. Carpini, *The Story of the Mongols,* p. 51.
48. Quoted in Christian, *A History of Russia, Central Asia, and Mongolia*, p. 405.
49. Quoted in Ratchnevsky, *Genghis Khan*, p. 152.

Chapter 6: Shamans and the Spirit World

50. Shaman South, "A Course in Mongolian Shamanism." www.geocities.com/Rain Forest/Vines/2146/mongolia/cms.htm, p. 5.
51. Shaman South, "A Course in Mongolian Shamanism," p. 6.
52. Shaman South, "A Course in Mongolian Shamanism," p. 6.
53. Shaman South, "A Course in Mongolian Shamanism," p. 6.
54. Shaman South, "A Course in Mongolian Shamanism," p. 4.
55. Anonymous, *The Secret History of the Mongols*, p. 37.
56. Quoted in Christian, *A History of Russia, Central Asia, and Mongolia*, p. 61.
57. Mircea Eliade, *Shamanism: Archaic Techniques of Ecstasy.* Trans. Willard R. Trask. Princeton, NJ: Princeton University Press, 1964, p. 29.
58. Morgan, *The Mongols,* p. 41.
59. Richard C. Foltz, *Religions of the Silk Road.* New York: St. Martin's Press, 1999, p. 120.

Chapter 7: Dancers, Wrestlers and Storytellers

60. Grousset, *The Empire of the Steppes*, p. 12.
61. Anonymous, *The Secret History of the Mongols*, pp. 13–14.
62. Polo, *The Travels*, p. 137.
63. Polo, *The Travels*, pp. 188–89.
64. Adam T. Kessler, *Empires Beyond the Great Wall: The Heritage of Genghis Khan.* Los Angeles: Natural History Museum of Los Angeles County, 1993, p. 155.
65. Quoted in Hilary Roe Metternich, *Mongolian Folktales.* Boulder, CO: Avery, 1996, pp. 18–20.
66. Quoted in Metternich, *Mongolian Folktales*, p. 14.
67. Anonymous, *The Secret History of the Mongols*, pp. 67–68.

For Further Reading

Kim Dramer, *Kublai Khan*. New York: Chelsea House, 1990. A concise biography of Genghis Khan's grandson, who founded the Yuan dynasty in China. This book is useful for its description of Mongol interaction with more advanced cultures.

Mary Hull, *The Mongol Empire*. San Diego: Lucent Books, 1998. A brief but comprehensive history of the empire that Genghis Khan built, with valuable references to daily life among the Mongol people.

Harold Lamb, *Genghis Khan*. Garden City, NY: Doubleday, 1927. A somewhat dated but nevertheless dramatic and readable account of the life of Genghis Khan and the great impact he had on Mongol life.

Stuart Legg, *The Heartland*. New York: Farrar, Straus & Giroux, 1970. A panoramic account of the peoples of the steppe, including the Mongols, and the impact they had on surrounding nations.

Paul Ratchnevsky, *Genghis Khan: His Life and Legacy*. Trans. Thomas Nivison Haining. Cambridge, MA: Blackwell, 1991. More up-to-date and scholarly than the biography by Lamb mentioned above, this story of Genghis's life is well told and contains a wealth of detail on how the Mongols lived.

Wendy Stein, *Shamans*. San Diego, CA: Greenhaven Press, 1991. This general survey of shamanistic practices around the world provides good background for the role the shamans played in Mongol life. The material on Siberian shamanism is especially relevant.

S. R. Turnbull, *The Mongols*. Oxford: Osprey, 1980. Part of a series called Men-at-Arms, this concise and easy-to-read book compresses much detail about Genghis Khan's army into a relatively few pages.

Works Consulted

Books

Anonymous, *The Secret History of the Mongols*. Trans. Francis Woodman Cleaves. Cambridge, MA: Harvard University Press, 1982. Difficult and obscure, this book was commissioned by Genghis Khan's son and successor Ogodei and written, in either 1228 or 1240, by an unknown scribe at his court. For advanced scholars, it is the ultimate source of much of the information available on Genghis's life and times.

Friar Giovanni DiPlano Carpini, *The Story of the Mongols Whom We Call the Tartars*. Trans. Erik Hildinger. Boston: Branden, 1996. An interesting account by a keen observer from the thirteenth century, exemplifying the terror the Mongols inspired in Europeans of that era.

David Christian, *A History of Russia, Central Asia, and Mongolia*, vol. 1, *Inner Eurasia from Prehistory to the Mongol Empire*. Cambridge, MA: Blackwell, 1998. An up-to-date and sweeping history of all the peoples of the steppe up to the time of Genghis Khan's Mongolia, with special emphasis on the economic background.

Mircea Eliade, *Shamanism: Archaic Techniques of Ecstasy*. Trans. Willard R. Trask. Princeton, NJ: Princeton University Press, 1964. Eliade, one of the world's leading students of religion and mythology, surveys the scope of shamanism as a worldwide aspect of primitive religion. He deals with the Mongols very selectively.

Richard C. Foltz, *Religions of the Silk Road*. New York: St. Martin's Press, 1999. A scholarly study of the cultural interaction along the Silk Road, the major east-west trade route linking Europe and the Orient during the Middle Ages.

Rene Grousset, *The Empire of the Steppes: A History of Central Asia*. Trans. Naomi Walford. New Brunswick, NJ: Rutgers University Press, 1970. An authoritative work, written by one of France's leading Mongolists, who presents a sympathetic account of the warlike character of the steppe nomads and relates the history of the Mongol Empire of Genghis Khan to earlier attempts at conquest by Central Asian tribes.

Charles J. Halperin, *Russia and the Golden Horde: The Mongol Impact on Medieval Russian History*. Bloomington: Indiana University Press, 1985. Devoted primarily to the activities of the Mongols on the western frontier of the empire, this book provides a detailed description of how Genghis and his successors dealt with conquered territories.

Adam T. Kessler, *Empires Beyond the Great Wall: The Heritage of Genghis Khan*. Los Angeles: Natural History Museum of Los Angeles County, 1993. A lavishly illustrated account of the history and culture of the Eurasian steppe.

Hilary Roe Metternich, *Mongolian Folktales*. Boulder, CO: Avery, 1996. A collection of Mongolian tales and fables, valuable not only in its own right, but also for the introduction by Pureviin Khorloo, a native Mongolian scholar and folklorist.

David Morgan, *The Mongols*. Malden, MA: Blackwell, 1986. This tightly written and very accessible book is part of a series entitled The Peoples of Europe. It deals concisely with many aspects of Mongol life, both during Genghis Khan's life and in the century or so following his death.

Marco Polo, *The Travels*. Trans. Ronald Latham. London: Penguin, 1958. An excellent translation of Marco Polo's account of his travels to the Orient and his stay at the court of Genghis Khan's grandson Kublai Khan. The style is conversational and the detail is rich, but Polo was prone to exaggeration.

Paul Ratchnevsky, *Genghis Khan—His Life and Legacy*. Trans. Thomas Nivison Haining. Cambridge, MA: Blackwell, 1991. Probably the best biography of Genghis Khan available, easy to read with plenty of insightful anecdotes.

Internet Sources

Shaman South, "A Course in Mongolian Shamanism." www.geocities.com/Rain Forest/Vines/2146/mongolia/cms.htm. This site contains interesting material on both the practice of Mongolian shamanism and the Mongols' religious beliefs in general.

Index

acrobats, 76

adoption practices, 22

adultery, 24, 31, 60 ——

afterlife, 67

alba tax, 37

alcoholic beverages, 51, 59

ancestor spirits, 51, 60, 62–63, 66–67

see also gods and spirits

arbans, 31

archery, 44, 53, 81

architecture, 77–78

armor, 42–43

army,

    achievements of, 41–42

    barbarity of, 47

    battle tactics of, 46–48

    body armor, 42–43

    discipline of, 45–46

    food rations, 44–45

    military training, 52–53

    organization of, 32

    rewards, 48–49

    warriors, 42

    weapons and gear, 43–44

art, 77–78

artifacts, 38, 77

artisans, 38

astrologers, 38, 72

astronomers, 38

basaq system, 37

battle gear, 43–44

    see also warfare

Batu, 83

Beleugetai (brother), 81

biliks (declarations), 34–36, 63

blitzkrieg, Mongol, 46

blood brotherhood alliances, 21, 27–29

body armor, 42–43

Borte (wife), 10, 11, 22, 33, 57, 60

bow and arrows, 42, 43, 44

bravery, 48–49

camels, 15, 16

cannibalism, 47, 54

Carpini, Friar Giovanni DiPlano, chronicles of, 12, 43, 44, 46, 53, 56, 60

cattle, 15, 16

cavalry soldiers, 42

Central Asian steppe, 11–12

Chagatai (son), 83

chief's, clan, 23–25, 31–32

children, 50, 52–53

Christian, David, 12, 14, 26, 30, 48, 54

Chungchen, 38

clan council meetings, 23–24

clans (*oboq*), 23–25

class distinctions, 25–26

climate, 11, 12

clothing, 16, 26

cosmos, regions of, 64–66

court, imperial, 33

    see also Mongolian Empire

creation story, 74

dancing, 75–77

daraugachis, 37

darkhans, 38–39

death, views of, 67

diet, 16, 54

dogs, 16, 53

drinking, 59

economic existence, 11, 18, 20, 21, 53

elderly, 50

Eliade, Mircea, 71

entertainers, 70–71, 75–77

Eternal Blue Heaven, 63

eternal life, 38

exogamy, 21, 55

falconry, 16, 81

family, 21–23, 50, 61

Father Sky, 63–64

folktales and fables, 74, 78–80

Foltz, Richard, 72

Gazan, 64

gender, 54

Genghis Khan

blood brotherhood alliances, 27–29

death of, 83

early life of, 10

as "first family," 60–61

interest in foreigners, 38

marriage to Borte, 10, 57, 60

military campaigns, 41–42, 50

oath of allegiance, 45–46

official pronouncements, 34–36, 63

rise to power, 8–9, 10–11

series of reforms, 30–40

tribes, 21, 29, 31–32

as warlord to emperor, 32–33

gers (homes), 16, 17, 33, 51–52

gifts, 39, 57

goats, 15, 16

Gobi Desert, 11

gods and spirits

ancestor worship, 51, 60, 62–63, 66–67

Father Sky, 63–64

Mother Earth, 64

religious faith, 72–73

three worlds and souls, 64–66

see also shamans

gold artifacts, 77

goldsmiths, 38

Great Khan. See Genghis Khan

Great Yasa, 30–31

Grousset, Rene, 13, 14, 31, 35, 75

guards, 36

Guyuk (grandson), 39–40

Halperin, Charles J., 32

Helegu (son), 84

herding and hunting practices, 11, 13–15

Hoelun (mother), 10, 61

homestead, 16, 17, 33, 51–52

horsemanship, 52, 81

horses

during battle, 44–45

importance of, 10, 15–16

lamellar armor for, 44

Mongol breed, 19

hunting

expeditions, 18–19

gear, 44

hygiene practices, 52, 60

imperial army, 32

see also army

imperial court, 33

imperial guards, 36

imperial secretariat, 36

inheritance, laws of, 22, 83

Innocent IV, Pope, 12, 15, 39–40

instruments, musical, 77

intertribal warfare, 24–25, 29

Ivan III, Czar, 83

jaghuns, 31

Jamuka, 10, 27–29, 47, 55

javelins, 43

Jochi (son), 83

jugglers, 76

Juvaini (Persian historian), 19, 21, 61

Juzjani (Indian chronicler), 69

Kaidu, 81

Karakorum, 35, 75, 78

Keeper of the Seal, 36

Picture Credits

Cover Photo: AKG
Art Resource, 46, 83
Art Resource/Werner Forman, 48, 63
Corbis/Adrian Arbib, 17
Corbis/Asian Art and Archaeology Inc., 39, 75
Corbis/Bettmann, 32, 45, 80
Corbis/Burnstein Collection, 28
Corbis/Dean Conger, 13, 15, 24, 53, 62, 78
Corbis/Earl and Nazima Kowall, 55

Corbis/Gregor Schmid, 11
Corbis/Brian Vikander, 43
Corbis/Nik Wheeler, 35, 71
FPG International, 14, 22
FPG International/Dennis Cox, 27
FPG International/Jean Kugler, 56
FPG International/Barry Rosenthal, 52
FPG International/Keren Su, 50, 51, 68
North Wind, 18, 66, 76
Stock Montage, 8, 31, 34, 37, 58, 69

About the Author

Robert Taylor has written on science, technology, history, politics, law, philosophy, medicine and contemporary culture. He lives in West Palm Beach, Florida.